AFTER THE EVENT

HUMAN RIGHTS ARE NOW FIRMLY ON THE AGENDA IN CHINA. Recent years have seen, for the first time, sustained criticism from outside governments of China's human rights record. This criticism has been carried directly to China's leaders by visiting heads of state and investigated more practically with the visits of independent human rights delegations from Australia, France and Canada. China, in response, has produced a white paper defending her record and has sent delegations of lawyers to the USA and Europe to investigate the mechanisms whereby human rights are protected and maintained in the West. This follows a long period during which the former USSR was under constant attack while China, which had an equally appalling record, mostly escaped criticism.

This collection deals with three main aspects of human rights in China • the question of rights — philosophical and practical • censorship in the PRC, state and self imposed • and China's dissident movement, in comparison with Eastern Europe and the former Soviet Union.

D0813144

AFTER
THE
EVENT

HUMAN RIGHTS
and their Future
IN CHINA

edited by
SUSAN WHITFIELD

wellsweep

This collection © The Wellsweep Press
Copyright in the individual essays remains with the authors.

First published in 1993 by
THE WELLSWEEP PRESS
1 Grove End House
150 Highgate Road
London NW5 1PD

in association with JUNE 4TH CHINA SUPPORT

Represented & Distributed in the UK & Europe by:
PASSWORD (BOOKS) LTD
serving independent literary publishers in the United Kingdom.
24 New Mount Street
Manchester M4 4DE

0 948454 18 0 paperback

BRITISH LIBRARY CATALOGUING-IN-PUBLICATION DATA
A catalogue record for this book is available from the British Library.

Designed and typeset by *wellsweep*
Printed and bound by E & E Plumridge

Editor's Preface

IN JUNE 1991, *June 4th China Support* organized an international conference on human rights in China, 'Rights in China: What Happens Next?' The conference was held in London over two days and attracted over 120 participants from Britain, Europe, the former Soviet Union and the USA.

The conference was divided into four main sessions: the Concept of Rights; Censorship; China and Eastern Europe and the Soviet Union; and China's International Role. There were also a number of seminars on various topics such as nationality issues and trade unions.

The paper presented by Jean-Pierre Cabestan in the final session has already been published in Lydie Koch-Miramond et al. eds., *La Chine et les droits de l'homme* (L'Harmattan, Paris 1991, pp. 80–96), and Ewa Brantley, the other speaker in this session, was unable to prepare her paper for publication due to illness. Therefore, only the papers from the first three sessions are published here.

I would like to thank all those who helped to make the conference such a success; those who helped with the organization, the chairpersons, speakers, and participants, the interpreter Wang Hao, and all those who generously gave financial support.

Details of the organization *June 4th China Support* are given after the index.

Susan Whitfield
London, 1992

CONTENTS

INTRODUCTION

ANDREW J NATHAN

CHINA IS POISED on the brink of change. But the forces for and against change momentarily hold one another in check.

The vitality of the economy is sapped by the inefficiency of state enterprises and the weakness of the state budget. Despite these problems the private-collective sector continues to grow rapidly. Local governments have made tacit bargains with central bureaucratic authorities which keep the centre in nominal control while leaving them with substantial economic and political authority.

The regime is widely unpopular. An elderly peasant said to a Chinese student of mine: 'We protected the communists from the nationalists and the Japanese, but we won't protect them next time.' The sister of another Chinese friend has a higher monthly income than ever before and more consumer possessions than her brother in New York, yet she complains bitterly about the administration of her unit, which she identifies with the communist system. Friends who work in government tell me that all their colleagues agree that Li Peng is incompetent. People watching television laugh at propaganda shows about the Party's benevolence to the people. A factory manager makes fun of the campaign to learn from Lei Feng, and there is a widespread sense that 'the system doesn't work.'

But these feelings are balanced by relative prosperity. Small businessmen complain one moment about corruption, then criticize the students who demonstrated in Tiananmen Square because they were endangering social order. They want change, but fear chaos that would make it impossible for entrepreneurs to survive.

Prosperity is uneven. Large parts of the population are underprivileged, including tens of millions of peasants below the poverty line, an estimated 60 to 100 million 'floating' workers, staff in loss-making enterprises, and most intellectuals, whose salaries have fallen behind those of factory workers and truck drivers. Just as China in 1964 was more prosperous than it had been for a long time yet harboured social cleavages which erupted into tremendous violence, the potential for violence today cannot be measured by the average per capita income or the number of televisions per household.

Passive resistance is widespread and includes slowdowns in the workplace. The regime's own media find ways to publish stories and essays refuting the official propaganda. Former Party General Secretary Zhao Ziyang sets the standard for passive resistance by refusing to admit his guilt for being too soft on the 1989 Tiananmen demonstrators. The existence of the democracy movement in exile in the US and Europe heightens the perception of the regime's fragility, as does the occasional headline-grabbing act of dissidence in China. Propaganda against the overseas democrats and against the West's alleged scheme of 'peaceful evolution' serves to maintain the impression of a beleaguered regime which has lost popular support and which is under attack with the cooperation of an ascendant capitalism.

The Chinese system is no longer totalitarian, but something more like traditional authoritarianism. People have no rights, but they are allowed some space. Such a regime survives partly because it is easier for most people to work their way round the controls than to oppose them. The stability of China now, such as it is, arises less from control than from the weakness of control.

Such a situation can only be temporary: a case of corruption, a miscarriage of justice, an incident arousing anti-foreign sentiment, a natural disaster, or action by a small group of oppositionists could each provide the spark for a major mass movement against the regime. But is likely to be the death of Deng Xiaoping rather than anything else which is the catalyst for the final events leading to the end of communism, and the crucial struggles will probably unfold among the top leaders, not in the arena of mass politics.

The leadership is split between those who wish to maintain the one-party system and those who wish to jettison it. The events of June 1989 polarized the difference between the two groups. For a long time the reformers believed that the communist system could be changed so as to incorporate freedom and democracy, while conservatives believed that a modicum of freedom could be permitted without threatening Party dominance. Both groups see their choices now in starker terms. Only Deng holds the two groups together, preventing each from moving against the other.

The events of June 1989 made the choice clear between preserving and jettisoning the system. They also demonstrated to all Chinese what none of them had known before — the extent of the regime's unpopularity. In a future crisis, each person will expect more opposition and less support for a regime than they expected prior to 1989.

Deng's crucial role in holding the regime together in 1989 must shake the confidence of the post-Deng leaders in their ability to cohere once he is gone. The reformers realize that if the hardliners continue to hold power after Deng dies, they will be treated more harshly than they were under Deng. The hardliners realize that is their rivals take power, they will not have Deng to protect them from retribution for the events of June 1989. Because 1989 removed any pretence that the hardliners and reformers disagree only over details in their quest for the same goal, each side has a strong incentive to preempt the other.

The weakness and ineffectuality of the post-June 4th crackdown will cause both pre- and anti-regime actors to estimate that a future democratic movement is more likely to succeed. Although scores were executed and thousands remain jailed after June 4th hundreds of others have been released, unrepentant. They have moral and even financial support among the stratum of managers in both private and state enterprises. Private business has become the refuge of disappointed reformers, who are building their political network along with their economic base. The 'civil society' that came to the fore in 1988–89 has not ceased to grow, although it is keeping quiet.

The failed 1991 Soviet coup set an example of the military refusing to support the hardline faction of a communist leadership. Each actor in the future Chinese drama will accordingly increase his estimate of the probability of a similar breakdown in the Chinese military hierarchy next time. After ten years of reform, the officer corps consists mostly of younger, better educated officers who are not doctrinaire. They favour politics of economic growth, and in the interests of stability they will throw their support behind whichever faction of the leadership appears most likely to win.

The post-coup events in the former Soviet Union, and post-communist elections in Bulgaria, Romania and Albania, showed how easily Communist Party members can survive under new party labels if they jump early enough from the old party's sinking ship. Such example will not only tempt Chinese Communist Party members to follow suit, but will also increase each Party member's estimate of the likelihood that other Party members will do so, and that the Party will then collapse.

Although the relatively weak foreign reaction to the Tiananmen events strengthened the hands of the conservative Chinese leaders, the subsequent strong reaction to the Soviet coup will have shaken their faith that the outside world will be equally disinterested next time they repress a popular movement. The impression of a worldwide tide against communism can become an independent force of its own, shaping the behaviour of politicians, just as a run on a bank or a stock market collapse shapes the behaviour of investors.

All these considerations have set up a new dynamic for the next power struggle within the regime. The struggle in May-June 1989, which Zhao Ziyang lost, was a struggle for the support of the older leaders and for possession of the historical mantle of Chinese communism. In the next struggle, the old leaders will be gone and the mantle of the Communist Party will be a liability rather than an asset.

Thanks to the monopoly of force and the absence of organized opposition, the regime can still survive if all its main leaders chose to stick together and resist pressure from below. But is is bound to collapse if a significant minority of them defect. To put it in terms of game theory, each actor's primary interest is for all of them to cooperate, but each actor's secondary interest is to defect first if there are going to be defections. The incentives for defection are therefore large, and there are costs for defecting late.

The interests of the elite actors, however, are not entirely symmetrical. A handful of conservatives tarred with the crime of June 4th are unable to defect from the communist coalition: their political fates are tied to its survival. Those who lost the battle of June 4th — Zhao Ziyang and his followers — can only return to power by denouncing the heritage of communism. The more neutral but pro-reform figures like Li Ruihuan and Zhu Rongji stand to benefit by separating themselves from the bloody part of this legacy. And those on the periphery of the regime, such as the military officers and provincial leaders, will gain by sitting on the sidelines until the trend becomes clear.

In effect, to stay in power, the hardliners will have to demonstrate that they can prevent any significant defections from the regime. This is a very difficult challenge in the aftermath of June 4th, Eastern Europe, and the Soviet collapse, and one they are likely to fail.

The probable breakdown of the regime from within means that another uprising on the scale of Tiananmen is not necessary for major change to occur. It has been argued that since even a movement as massive as that of 1989 could not overthrow the regime, and since the regime punished the participants in the movement, it will be impossible to get such a huge movement going again. Even it this is true, a much smaller movement than that of 1989 can spark a round of defections within the regime. Indeed, the death of Deng without any immediate mass response may lead to the same effect.

If the Chinese Communist Party crumbles, what difference is it going to make? The situation today bears a strong resemblance to that near the end of the Qing dynasty in the first decade of this century. The Qing reformed, looked strong, repressed the opposition, and then suddenly disappeared in a whiff of gunsmoke when its officials started to defect. After the Qing, Yuan Shikai emerged in power — a member of the old regime, espousing a new ideology but ruling though the old bureaucracy.

The same is likely to happen in post-Deng China. The democratic movement in exile does not represent a viable alternative as a government, there is no well-established Solidarity-type movement and no long-established opposition group as in Taiwan: the new rulers can only come from within the old ruling party. In Eastern Europe and the former Soviet Union, not only leaders but many other elements of the old system survived, such as the state-owned enterprises, the military and the police. In China, the fall of communism is not likely quickly to change the unit (*danwei*) system, the system of state grain procurement and distribution, or the household registration system. The elite of cadre-intellectuals with its network of relationships and sense of a mandate to rule will still be in place all over the country. Perhaps most importantly, given the already considerable authority of local governments (some of which are quite popular), the collapse of the regime in Beijing will not necessarily bring much change to government or daily life in provinces like Guangdong or Sichuan.

In one sense, the collapse of communism will be merely a change of label that occurs at one stage during a long evolutionary process. In another sense, the communist regime has already all but disappeared. Broad forces are working themselves out regardless of the fates of Li Peng, the Chinese Communist Party, and Marxism-Leninism-Mao Zedong Thought. Already only 20% of the Chinese receive state subsidies, the remainder living entirely off the market. By some estimates the non-state sector accounts for 80% of agricultural production, 50% of commerce, and 40% of industrial output. When the central government launched a nationwide 'socialist education movement' in the summer of 1991, local officials in some places used the occasion to spur backward villages to develop commercial enterprise. In intellectual and academic life, communism counts for nothing and in political struggles and policy decisions, it serves only as a rationalization. The hardliners preside over a society they do not control.

Political changes will shape the future of rights in China, but the decisive role will be played by Chinese who have thought carefully about what rights are, why they are needed in China, and the nature of the obstacles to their realization. Such an enquiry should be international because the issues are universal and because, for the time being, they cannot be freely discussed in China.

In June 1991, *June 4th China Support* organized a conference in London to discuss human rights and the situation in China. The presenters were a varied group, including academics and non-academics, China specialists and non-specialists. The papers, which are published in this volume, presented a variety of fresh views by people of broad experience in a number of areas.

The first set of papers addresses the concept of human rights itself. Are human rights a universal value or do they vary from culture to culture? Are the same rights of equal priority everywhere? Are rights an end in themselves or a means to some other goal?

Jay Bernstein accepts some of the criticisms which have been directed at human rights' philosophies in both China and the West: that no proof can be given for the existence of such rights, and that there is no way to protect them outside a political community. He presents a rationale for rights which should be widely acceptable to Chinese as well as to Westerners: rights are 'the necessary conditions for effective participation in community life.' By treating rights as a means to an end, but an end which is today accepted throughout the world, he contributes to bridging the culture gap that sometimes frustrates discussion of rights between China and the West.

James Seymour accepts an instrumental view of rights for the purposes of argument. He argues that the movement that fights for such rights must abandon the paternalism characteristic of intellectuals, and should give equal priority to the rights of workers and peasants. He also reports on North American 'Community Based Organizations' which work for rights in China separately from the better-known exile democracy groups.

The hypothesis that rights are related to democracy is subjected to empirical test by Chan Hong-mo and his colleagues from *The Alliance for a Better China*. The team complied data on the level of democracy in 164 states and correlated this measure with various measures of human rights. Despite the inevitable crudeness of such an effort, strong positive correlations were revealed in every test. This does not tell us whether rights are needed for democracy or vice versa, but it supports the view that the two are linked.

The second section addresses censorship — one of the primary mechanisms whereby governments deprive people of their rights. Chinese censorship has been misunderstood because it does not operate through a specialized bureaucracy and does not concentrate on blocking publication of certain statements. Michael Schoenhals shows that Chinese censorship instead functions through the pro-active leadership of the Party's Propaganda Department over editors and publishers, who are themselves Party members, and thereby aims to get certain things said. Bonnie McDougall develops this point by showing how the mechanisms of Party control lead to self-censorship, which is politically more effective than negative censorship. The literary results of self-censorship however, are mixed: it impoverishes many texts but for some writers creates an opportunity for deeper and more universal writing. Lucie Borota concludes this section by analyzing Chinese press coverage of the overthrow of communism in Czechoslovakia in 1989. Torn between the need to comment on facts that its readers knew from other sources, and the desire to deny the unpleasant substance of these facts, the official newspaper *Renmin Ribao* (People's Daily) presented coverage that was slow, fragmentary and confusing.

The third set of papers compares China with Eastern Europe and the former Soviet Union. Liu Binyan explores some reasons why Chinese intellectuals have been less active in opposing the dictatorship of the Party than their counterparts elsewhere. Yuri Garushyants pays tribute to the ability of Chinese dissidents suffering repression to come up with a strong rationale for human rights in the late 1970s, but points out that, despite reform in China, the values of totalitarianism are still in place not only among the elderly leaders but among many of the people as well.

The world waits for the next phase of change in China. All our futures are to some extent involved, because of China's vast size and impact on our planet and because of the contributions the Chinese can make by thought and experience to the storehouse of human wisdom. The thoughtful papers collected in this volume add to our understanding of what is to come.

THE CONCEPT
OF RIGHTS

THE THEORY AND PRACTICE OF HUMAN RIGHTS

JAY BERNSTEIN

TODAY HUMAN RIGHTS are a focus of attention as, perhaps, they have never been before.[1] Human rights activities, both political and legal, are growing and solidifying in a context where we are being made continually aware — both through the media and through the efforts of organizations like Amnesty International — of the violation of the rights of innumerable persons and groups throughout the world. In a time when the values and goals of socialism in its traditional political guise are significantly on the wane, a good deal of the socialist agenda is reappearing as a series of human rights claims: welfare rights, workers' rights, rights to education and health care, and the like. For the time being at least, socialist and humanitarian ideals are surviving most significantly, that is in ways that politically matter, within the discourse and practice of human rights.

Yet we cannot remain either sanguine or satisfied with this situation, for within this flurry of rights activity and awareness there exists, if not silence, then disarray in the philosophical interrogation of rights. That is, within the project seeking to determine *what* rights are and *how* they are to be founded. Indeed, it is tempting to say that the philosophical articulation of rights — the project of determining their meaning, foundation, scope, and the criteria for identifying and individuating them — exists in inverse proportion to their political dispersion and growth. To admit this is to admit that we do not as yet have a firm rational basis for pursuing rights and attempting to protect and uphold the rights claims of ourselves and others. And to the degree to which we lack this rational basis we must lack as well rational confidence in our political endeavours insofar as they are oriented by the desire to promote human rights. Certainly, however, it is just that desire that has brought us together today. Most of us here believe

[1] This is an elaborated version of a talk given at the conference, 'Rights in China: What Happens Next?' held in London in June 1991. While some of the argumentation in this paper only emerged in the course of writing up the talk, I have tried to maintain some of the flavour of the original oral presentation. I offer a somewhat different construction of the ideas presented here in my paper 'Right, Revolution and Community: Marx's "On the Jewish Question"', in Peter Osborne, ed. *Socialism and the Limits of Liberalism* (Verso Press, London 1991), pp. 91–119.

that what happened in Tiananmen Square in June 1989 was a gross and absolute violation of the human rights of the protesters. Certainly what happened there was an atrocity, but was that atrocity a violation of human rights or something else?

ABOUT RIGHTS

Rights, especially human rights, have always had a rough ride within philosophy. The classical objections to (natural) rights put by Burke, Bentham and Marx — three thinkers whose political and theoretical orientations are as different as they could be — are still looking pretty unanswerable.[1] To concede the power of their arguments is not, however, to deny that people have rights or that those rights matter. What Burke, Bentham and Marx denied is the existence of *natural* rights, the 'Rights of Man' defended by the French revolutionaries, and the sorts of rights that people were claimed to have as such, irrespective of any natural, social or political allegiances. My strategy in what follows will be to suggest that the classical arguments against natural rights have substance, but that substance only goes as far as our understanding of the foundations of rights. Once we are clear about the nature and foundation of rights are we shall then be able to make a case for human rights. This case may well turn out to be weaker than many human rights activists have thought or hoped; nonetheless, what remains of human rights will be rational and defensible, something that can be striven after with understanding and confidence.

Let us say that a person has a right X means, very roughly, that someone or all others have a duty to let that person do or have X. The existence of such a duty gives the person with the right a claim against one or all others with respect to X. X can be a negative liberty (like free speech or religious belief), or a positive good (like food, shelter, or health care). In other words, to say that a person has a right is just to say that someone or all others are under an *obligation* to satisfy that right, and therefore, within the language of rights, rights and duties are logically bound together. So understood, rights are 'stronger' than fundamental needs or objective interests. For example, a person may indeed need food in order to survive, but in acknowledging that need we are not committed to acknowledging that someone or all others are obligated to satisfy that need. Of course, we may think the existence of needs or objective interests is a good moral *basis* for ascribing rights to the individuals concerned, but nothing in the logical language of

[1] For the relevant texts and commentary see Jeremy Waldron, ed., *Nonsense Upon Stilts: Bentham, Burke and Marx on the Rights of Man* (Methuen, London 1987).

needs or interest yields the entailment relations that would connect them with the duties of others.

Rights are like needs and interests in that they are directed toward or range over the same sorts of items. Rights, we might say, are needs or interests which are accorded a special significance. The significance that needs and interests acquire when they become rights (or are regarded as rights) passes over directly to the right holder. Because rights and duties are logically bound together, a person possessing rights is *entitled* to make claims against those who are under an obligation to satisfy those claims. That entitlement empowers the right holder, making them a person of dignity, not a petitioner dependent on the benevolence of others. Again, the comparison with needs is instructive. When others around me have needs, I may well feel sufficient benevolence towards them to provide the aid they require. And if I offer charity, then I reasonably expect its beneficiary to feel gratitude. Such is not the case with rights. If others have rights claims with respect to me, then I have an obligation to do what is required in order to satisfy that claim: and its being a rights claim means that the right holder is so stationed with respect to me that *only* he or she can release me from the obligation that the right claim entails.

The possession of rights logically entails corresponding duties for others, and as a consequence, the holders of a right possess a social standing, a dignity they would not have if they only had a need. Dignity or empowerment is a significant social good, and formally, at least, the possession of rights is *constitutive* of this good. In a modern society one is legally and morally empowered only through the possession of rights (and not through status, as was the case in pre-modern societies); but if rights are constitutive of empowerment, being without rights must deprive individuals of such empowerment.[1] All this is implied by the definition of rights, a definition, I am contending, that captures most of the appeal of rights discourse and leads us to believe that rights matter. Weakly stated, and for the moment ignoring the question of foundation, human rights are such in virtue of their scope; they are rights had by everyone irrespective of status or special relation, eg. being the citizen of a state, a party to a contract, or a member of a voluntary organisation.

[1] The thesis that rights are constitutive of empowerment in modern states was suggested to me by the late Deborah Fitzmaurice. Without her guidance and help this paper would have been more severly flawed than it undoubtedly is.

RIGHTS, MACHINERY AND MAGIC

If we understand rights in the manner suggested by my, uncontentious, definition, then it is easy to understand why various rights documents like the United Nations Declaration have been found so attractive. If there really are human rights, then it looks as if they alone could deliver all that is most significant in acknowledging the dignity of human beings and, alone, they could provide support for the most important values that moral and political philosophers have been seeking to defend since the time of the Greeks. It is therefore surprising that the defence of human rights has not been at the centre of work in moral and political philosophy over the past 150 years.

In order to understand this state of affairs we should begin prior to the point where the problems begin. There are, and no one doubts that there are, legal, positive rights. These rights are embedded in and protected by law, and thus are immersed in the massive machinery of the legal system — legislative bodies, courts, police, special agencies — that exist to promulgate rights and to make sure that those who have duties fulfill them. The machinery of the legal system replaces the logical link between rights and duties with a complex social institution. Or, to put it a better way, the legal system exists for the sake of sustaining the bond between rights and duties. The legal system of a democratic polity just *is*, I am tempted to say, the social and institutional instantiation of rights discourse.

But legal rights are not what grabs the interest in rights discourse, especially human rights discourse. What makes rights seem so important is the belief that there are moral rights: rights which people have independently of being given them by law-makers, special agencies or anyone else. Nor is it accidental that we should believe that it is moral rights rather than legal rights which matter. One wants moral rights because they are counters against legal systems which have been designed unjustly or which fail to support the obligations they officially sanction. Possessing rights would seem to matter most at precisely the point where their legal inscription ends, at the point where the legal system cannot be relied upon to do the work of promulgating the rights we think we have, or protecting the rights we have been formally said to have.

Of course, there are circumstances in which we can easily conceive of what it would be for people to be possessed of moral rights. Above all, such rights fit in naturally with a theological picture of the universe in which persons are the creations and ultimate property of a benevolent god who is regarded as the Legislator. If all or nearly all believed in the existence of such a god, then they would have good reasons for believing in the existence of moral rights. But that set of circumstances is not ours, and hence the question must arise as to whether we can make sense of moral rights outside of a theological account? There are serious grounds for doubt. As Alasdair MacIntyre has stated:

> ...there are no such [human or natural] rights, and belief in them is one with belief in witches and unicorns. The best reasons for asserting so bluntly that there are no such rights is indeed precisely the same type as the best reason we possess for asserting there are no witches and the best reason we possess for asserting there are no unicorns: every attempt to give good reasons for believing there *are* such rights has failed.[1]

In assimilating moral rights to witches and unicorns MacIntyre is drawing our attention to how puzzling rights appear when we attempt to think of them as natural or *a priori* properties of human beings: things human beings possess independently of their social interactions with others.

What, we may ask, makes arguing for rights so difficult? Our analysis of the nature of rights and our discrimination between legal and moral rights give us good clues as to where the difficulty lies. To argue for moral rights is to demonstrate that the logical link between rights and duties exists as a moral relation between persons independently of their wills; and hence that people are empowered without any person or group empowering them. Even on the surface, this appears to be an odd claim. While it is not difficult to imagine that everyone is obligated not to interfere with others with regard to negative liberties, it is almost impossible to imagine everyone having rights to goods (food, shelter, etc.) since, in the abstract, it would remain utterly indeterminate as to who was obligated to satisfy the claim legitimated by a right. But to say someone has a right but that no one person or group is obligated to satisfy the entailed obligation is, given the definition of a right, contradictory. One might say that everyone is obligated to fulfill a right holders' claim; but the staunchest defenders of rights do not believe that. Further, if it is conceded that a significant element in the possession of a right is the way it empowers the holder, then it makes no sense to believe in moral rights since empowerment is a social and not a natural good.

If my way of discriminating legal and moral rights is sound, then it becomes tempting to say that the relation between rights and duties is a social

---

[1] Alasdair MacIntyre, *After Virtue* (Duckworth, London 1981), p. 67.

one, and that arguments for moral rights seek to displace this with a logical relation. Typically then, theories of moral rights attempt to argue from the fact that, if I am to pursue any projects, I (instrumentally) must have certain things, like rational agency, to the thesis that I (logically and/or morally) must have a right to these things.[1] To see what is wrong with this argument — in its leap from what I instrumentally must have to what I logically or morally claim — we need only look at an analogous argument. If there are certain things I must have as a necessary condition for me to pursue any projects whatsoever, then I have good reasons for wanting a system of rights that will secure those things. My hunch is that, in the original argument, the logical and/or moral 'must' is standing in for an instrumental 'must' and attempting to 'upgrade' an ordinary piece of instrumental reasoning. The only reason I would have for thinking that I must have certain rights is because possessing them is (under certain conditions) a necessary means to my pursuing my ends. Under different circumstances, different means might be necessary: for example, having the status of a lord and not a serf, or being the member of one caste rather than another. So the philosopher's moral 'must' is just the transformation of a contingent, practical and social connection into a logical connection.

The philosopher's argument is fallacious because no justification is given for the movement from the instrumental to the moral 'must', the argument simply transforms the former into the latter. And, while the premise of the argument refers to items that can legitimately be said to exist independently of any particular set of social arrangements, the conclusion refers to a very specific social form. My practical recasting of the argument underlines this fact. Thus the most that pure argument could show is that (under certain social conditions) only by being a rights holder can I secure the goods I need in order to pursue any projects I might have. But from this it does not follow that I am as such a right holder or that I am entitled to make rights claims. It is a practical means-ends argument only.

The philosopher replaces the legal and political machinery that makes rights work with the magic of a logical relation. The hard lesson that rights involve machinery is a political lesson that Hannah Arendt drew from the experience of refugees during and after the Second World War.[2] Arendt traces the origin of what I am terming the philosopher's conception of rights back to their emergence where, 'in the new secularized and

---

[1] The most notable modern defense of moral rights is offered in Alan Gewirth, *Reason and Morality* (University of Chicago Press, 1978).
[2] Hannah Arendt, *The Origins of Totalitarianism* (The World Publishing Company, New York 1958). All page references in the text are to this edition.

emancipated society, men were no longer sure of these social and human rights which until then had been outside the political order and guaranteed not by government and constitution, but by social, spiritual and religious forces' (p. 291). As a consequence, she continues, 'throughout the nineteenth century, the consensus of opinion was that human rights had to be invoked whenever individuals needed protection against the new sovereignty of the state and the new arbitrariness of society.' This required regarding man himself as both the source as well as the ultimate goal of rights and laws. What we saw as the tension involved in the distinction between legal and moral rights, Arendt perceives as a paradox: 'From the beginning the paradox involved in the declaration of inalienable human rights was that it reckoned with an "abstract" human being who seemed to exist nowhere, for even savages lived in some kind of social order.'

What I am calling the 'hard lesson' that rights involve machinery, Arendt states in these bold terms: 'The Rights of Man, after all, had been defined as "inalienable" because they were supposed to be independent of all government: but it turned out that the moment human beings lacked their own government and had to fall back upon their minimum rights, no authority was left to protect them and no institution was willing to guarantee them' (pp. 291–2). During this century, non-governmental organizations have been founded with the express intention of doing for minorities and refugees what no government body appeared willing to do. But, at least at the time of the writing of *The Origins of Totalitarianism* in 1949–50, Arendt could state without challenge that not only were governments opposed to the encroachment on their sovereignty represented by the efforts of such organizations, but that the 'concerned nationalities themselves did not recognize a non-national guarantee, mistrusted everything which was not clear-cut support for their "national" (as opposed to mere "linguistic, religious, and ethnic") rights, and preferred either, like the Germans and Hungarians, to turn to the protection of the "national" mother country, or, like the Jews, to some kind of interterritorial solidarity'. Events in 1989 in Eastern Europe make this statement more rather than less true.

Rights, for Arendt, are only intelligible within a political setting, within some form of human community where it is at least possible for individuals to fight for and assert their freedom. For this reason, she regards living under tyranny as preferable to living nowhere, having no identifiable enemy and no community against which demands can be made. Only participation in the community makes having or losing rights matter: 'Not the loss of specific rights, then, but the loss of community willing and able to guarantee any rights whatsoever, has been the calamity which has befallen ever-increasing numbers of people. Man, it turns out, can lose all so-called Rights of Man without losing his essential quality as man, his human dignity. Only the loss of polity itself expels him from humanity' (p. 297).

Arendt ends her discussion of human rights and the Rights of Man with these words. Given their force and eloquence, I shall quote this passage in full.

> The great danger arising from the existence of people forced to live outside the common world is that they are thrown back, in the midst of civilisation, on their natural givenness, on their mere differentiation. They lack that tremendous equalizing of differences which comes from being citizens of some commonwealth and yet, since they are no longer allowed to partake in the human artifice, they begin to belong to the human race in much the same way as animals belong to a specific animal species. The paradox involved in the loss of human rights is that such a loss coincides with the instant when a person becomes a human being in general — without a profession, without a citizenship, without an opinion, without a deed by which to identify and specify himself — *and* different in general, representing nothing but his own absolutely unique individuality which, deprived of expression within and action upon a common world, loses all significance. (p. 302)

RIGHTS AND POLITICAL COMMUNITY

If we are to pursue the leads given by our refutation of the philosopher's conception of rights and Arendt's historico-political analysis, then we must attempt to make sense of rights as entities essentially bound up with some political form of community. On its own, however, this is not enough. Once we agree that legal rights are the correct model for an understanding of rights in general, then we must face the dilemma that the appeal of rights is that they weigh against *mere* legality, against laws that fail to recognise negative liberties or positive goods. So we want legal rights as a model, but we do not wish to be positivistic about such rights; we require a 'moral' moment to delimit legality. Although consistently viewed as an opponent of rights, in fact the most perspicuous representation of a conception of rights along the lines indicated by our analysis here is to be found in an early essay of Marx's, 'On the Jewish Question'.[1]

Marx's essay provides an analysis of the various declarations that emerged from the American and French Revolutions which reveals that these declarations are shaped by a dual conception of society. Modern societies, Marx contends, are divided into two primary spheres of activity: the state and the political practices attending it on the one hand, and civil society with its domains of economic activity and private life on the other. This dual conception of society, which Marx reads as the historical consequence of the collapse of the feudal order, maps directly on to a dual conception of rights: political rights or the rights of the citizen (tracking the domain of the state), and the Rights of Man which belong to individuals as members of civil society. These latter rights include the familiar rights to property, security and the like. In broad terms. Marx thinks that all morally significant elements of rights belong to the domain of the state, while all the morally dubious aspects of rights find their place in civil society. However, he simultaneously contends that civil society is the basis of society as a whole. The following well-known passage provides a good indication of the basic elements of Marx's dualistic conception of the relation between state and civil society.

> The perfected political state is by its nature the species-life of man in opposition to his material life. All the presuppositions of this egoistic life continue to exist outside the sphere of the state in civil society, but as qualities of civil society. Where the political state has attained its full degree of development man leads a double life, a life in heaven and a life on earth, not only in his mind, in his consciousness, but in reality. He lives in the political community where he regards himself as a communal being, and in civil society, where he is active as a private individual, regards other men as means, debases himself to a means and becomes a plaything of alien powers... Man in his immediate reality, in civil society, is a profane being... In the state, on the other hand, where he is considered a species being, he is the imaginary member of a fictitious sovereignty, he is divested of his real individual life and filled with an unreal universality. (p. 220)

The distinction Arendt draws between life within and life outside community Marx regards as adumbrated within the structure of modern soci-

[1] Karl Marx, *Early Writings*, translated by Rodney Livingstone and Gregory Benton (Penguin Books, Harmondsworth, Middlesex 1975), pp. 211–241. All page references are to this edition.

eties themselves. Because life in civil society structurally requires that individuals take only an instrumental relation to their world, then life within civil society is ordered *as if* our relations to others was utterly contingent, *as if* we were natural and not social beings, and *as if* the determinate relations regulating our behaviour within civil society were the spontaneous products of our immediate interests and desires rather then products of historical development. The qualification of the life of civil society by these three 'as ifs' lends force and plausibility to the view that rights belong to man as such; this view arose as a consequence of the belief that the deposed feudal order of society had clothed the natural life of man in the mythic garb of religious belief. Against the background of the new science and analogous developments, it seemed plausible to believe that the overcoming of the feudal order revealed the real, *natural* foundation for social life.

So the disposition and content of rights which articulate the legal relations of individuals in civil society as portrayed in the first rights declarations came to parallel the fiction that market economies are the spontaneous product of a wholly 'natural' human activities. As a consequence, Marx contends, these rights do not go beyond 'egoistic man, man as a member of a civil society, namely an individual withdrawn into himself, his private interest and his private desire and *separated* from community' (p. 230). Of course, the actual content of such separation from community is itself social or communal in character, for example, private property rights, above all, rights to private ownership over the means of production. While in other contexts Marx disputes the justice of economies organized around private production and market exchange, here the focus of his attack is against the fiction that such an organization of economic life and the rights that hold that organization in place can any sense be regarded as 'natural' or 'immediate'. Private production and ownership are no more 'natural' than collective production and tribal ownership. Both are social forms of production and ownership underwritten by different social values and rules.

More importantly, the rights that individuals possess as members of civil society are guaranteed and underwritten by the state, that is, even if the Rights of Man belong to men only as members of civil society, the legitimizing and protecting of those rights is something the political community does, something it takes to be its responsibility, and therefore something we collectively take to be our responsibility; it is something *we* do. It is for this reason that Marx looks to political rights, the rights of men as citizens, where being a citizen defines our sense of both community and our membership in it, for his understanding of the true nature of rights. About these, he says, they are 'only exercised in community with others', and 'their content is participation in community' (p. 227). The best way to conceive of Marx's idea here is to regard it as providing a reformulation of rights, one which *a fortiori* challenges the abstract definition with which we started by revealing its suppressed social content; rights are political, can only be exercised in community, and have participation in community as their content.

Because rights essentially involve corresponding duties, they can only be exercised in community; which is to say, unless there are agencies for fulfilling the corresponding obligations rights entail, or for protecting those rights which everyone has an obligation to fulfill, then talk of rights (as opposed to needs, interests, wants or goods) will be empty. People only have these rights, and hence the opportunity to exercise them, when they are regarded as members of the community. Thus the possession of rights is co-extensive with membership in the community: one is not a full member of a (modern) community unless and until such time as she or he possesses the rights that define membership. Someone's possession of rights defines our recognition of him or her as a member of our community, and communal membership without rights would be formal and empty. It is just this thought that explains why empowerment has come to be constituted by rights. If possessing rights constitutes full membership in the community, then one lacks a social identity that matters until one possesses rights. But once one has the requisite rights, then for modern societies one possesses all that is significant in way of membership. Rights define communal membership against other criteria, such as race, religion and language.

But this suggestion only works if the content of such rights provides for the necessary (if not sufficient) conditions for effective participation in community; the right to vote, assemble, hold office, and so on. Political rights do more than 'protect' the political sphere: they constitute the range of activities that make individuals into political agents. It is only insofar as one can vote, hold office, etc. that one is a political agent with a place in the political community, a community formed by the totality of agents and the instituted political activities. If we now consider how community and participation interact in this definition, we can see why Marx emphasizes political community. Marx's insistence on participation is meant to show that rights range over *activities* — that rights communities are defined by their activities, and not by blood, belief or language — and that rights communities are communities of will and are created, subject to reason and decision, and not given.

It is because they are communities of will that explains why rights communities must be democratic; communities in which full membership necessarily involves having some say over the future and fate of the community. If they were not democratic then communal life would be constituted by something other than the activities of its members. The bond between community and activity can only be realised if membership, and the empowerment that follows from such membership, can have an effect on the existence and nature of the community. If empowerment was restricted to acting *in* the community but not on it, then the community itself would exist outside the activities of its members and, this being the case, its existence and nature would be a 'given', a natural item, and hence in contradiction with its 'active' content.

Having strengthened the role of will in the definition of modern community, it may appear as if Marx will be forced to return to the social contract tradition which the centring of community in his account of rights is designed to displace. But this would be to misunderstand the degree to which Marx is acknowledging the importance of freedom bequeathed by the liberal tradition in judging political community to be its fullest articulation. The individualism of civil society falls below this level of articulation by making the goal of political association the preservation of civil society (p. 231). The fictional naturalness of the Rights of Man 'leads each man to see in other men not the *realization* but the *limitation* of his own freedom' (p. 230). This sentence provides us with the metaphysical thesis underlying Marx's analysis as well as the moral motive which I suggested earlier would be necessary if rights were not to be reduced to mere legality.

To claim that human freedom is only realized in community with others is just to say that the mere capacity to act freely — that is in accordance with the philosopher's thought that to act freely is being able to have acted otherwise — tells us nothing about actual freedom. Actual freedom is defined by opportunities that only become available in society: having a say in the political future of one's community, choosing to live here rather than there, choosing this rather than that work, having a say in the conditions under which one works, and so on. Marx's emphasis on community is not opposed to individuals; rather, as was clear in the case of private property, it underlies how the possibilities for individual freedom and action are socially constituted. The reductive character of the rights Marx objects to does not derive from investing individuals with rights to do certain things and prohibiting others or even the state itself from interfering with those rights. Freedom to vote, form parties and to have a free press all define and protect the political process, a communal process that exists through the activities of individuals and voluntary groups of individuals. The Rights of Man are reductive because they are conceived of as rights against the community as such, as if the range of activities and freedoms that individuals in society possess were available prior to and independently of the particular society they inhabit. It is to suppose that in achieving one's own ends one is acting independently of the community. But such independence is a socially constituted and sanctioned practice, something unique to our form of life. One is independent not in opposition to others but through and in relation to them. This is the suppressed sociality and universality underpinning the fictional naturalness and egoism of civil society.

To say that the content of rights is participation in community is just to say that rights are teleological. To reiterate, they constitute the necessary conditions for effective participation in communal life. To extend this analysis from political society to civil society would end up giving us just those positive goods that condition life in civil society: education, food, housing, the right to work, and so forth. We value these things because they either constitute social life or provide the necessary conditions that must be satisfied if full participation in the life of society is to be possible. While we may think that no man or beast should starve when there exists sufficient in the world to feed all, this moral view is not what is at issue here. What rights constitute and protect is membership in 'this' community; and to have full membership is to be empowered to a degree to which one can participate in the full range of activities that collectively define social life for us. This is why contemporary rights theory often begins with the undefended premise that rights guarantee equal respect and/or equal opportunity. These doctrines, I am suggesting, are derivative from that of effective participation in communal life.

Since we intend that participation in civil life flow from the individuals constituting it, then we want to insure that such individuality is adequately supported. Such support would not only involve the sorts of items that now go under the heading of 'equal opportunity', but almost certainly some of the existing list of negative liberties. Negative liberties, like positive goods, feature on our list of rights because they contribute to a certain modern, democratic and free form of life, otherwise we would have no grounds for considering them. They exist in virtue of this form of life and owe nothing to man as such. Rights matter because they constitute and protect the range of activities that just are the life of modern, socialized individuals. Having rights makes their possessor a full member of the community of which he or she is a part. Such an individual is 'free' in that they are able to participate in the full range of activities that matter to the community, and possess all the relevant choices which the community can offer.

HUMAN RIGHTS

At this point a difficult question arises: is the moral motive of Marx's analysis, viz. the realization of human freedom through participation in community, sufficient to inhibit a slippage from right to mere legality? One pertinent way of focussing this question would be to ask the further question: what is to be the fate of those who are unrecognized, those who have not been given the rights constitutive of full membership in the community?

As a matter of fact, we know that the way in which minority groups, and the individuals belonging to such groups, have attained their rights is through political and legal struggle. So in asking the question about the fate of such groups we are asking after the *moral* basis for such struggles and the moral grounds, if any, that might justify an existing community in refusing claims for such rights. The most fundamental moral basis for a claim to rights by a minority group is that there is no significant difference, ie. no morally relevant difference, between its members and those who already possess full rights. It is here that the contention that rights range over activities comes into its own. It follows from this that rights communities are communities of action — self-determining communities defined by actions constitutive of community membership. It thus follows that all that is relevant to determining potential membership in the community is the capacity to perform the relevant actions. This is the historical discovery and presupposition of modernity. By conceiving of community in terms of (self-determining) activity, all the standard forms of exclusion — race, sex and class — immediately drop out of consideration. What tends to reveal that individuals have the capacity to perform the range of activities constitutive of full participation in community is that the fundamental prerequisities for performing the specific action types at issue are displayed and revealed in performing the most routine social actions. All the potential that would make slaves full citizens was already revealed in slave life and the kinds of obedience required in it; all that would justify giving women the vote was already displayed in the political struggle that eventuated in it. Everyday practice is a communal practice, a practice whose (potential and actual) symmetries and reversibilities of position demonstrate that those participating in it already implicitly recognise one another as members of the same community. So rights struggles initiate a movement from implicit and potential communal membership to explicit and actual membership.

Implicit membership is revealed in the linguistic and social practices the excluded group are allowed to perform, which in turn forms the ground for the ascription of potentiality for their performing the activities from which they have been excluded. Such shifts from implicit and potential to explicit and actual manifest how rights, literally, empower and dignify those previously excluded through their realization of their freedom.

Sometimes rights struggles involve not just the giving of standing rights to new and different groups of individuals, but the struggle for new rights. The moral basis for these struggles is that the rights being struggled for range over items that are tacitly or implicitly already recognized by the community as being necessary for full and effective participation. The right to education is a good example. While the original members of a community may not have considered this a sphere of right because they were all educated already and their not being so was socially improbable, the widening of the community came to reveal that what had been taken for granted as in fact something without which a certain range of activities could not be fully and effectively performed, and also that it was not something that could be taken for granted.

It is because the moral basis for rights does not make specific reference to historically determinate characteristics of people (like their beliefs), nor what would naturally differentiate them from others (skin colour or sex), it becomes comprehensible why it was thought that rights themselves were natural. Such a move conflates rights with the grounds of their ascription or refusal. The universalizing movement that restricts the claims of mere legality by weighing against it human action and freedom does not, however, show rights themselves to be separable from the communities that promulgate and enforce them.

This communitarian and political conception of rights thus leaves human rights dangling, but less than one might have thought. Human rights are only 'manifesto' rights; rights we (morally) believe all humans ought to have. To say this is not to claim that human beings all have a right to rights but rather to claim, first, that we have come to believe that no-one could effectively participate in any conceivable modern human community unless they had the rights laid down in, for example, the United Nations Charter. Human rights are the minimum body of rights necessary for any community to be a rights community, and this because they designate the minimum necessary conditions which would permit individuals to operate in a truly (self-determining) social world. Secondly, we recognize that the moral basis upon which we are right holders owes nothing to our specific qualities and characteristics, and that since possessing rights enables us to enjoy those liberties and goods constitutive of the only form of life we find morally choice-worthy, then there are no grounds for denying that others ought to enjoy such rights. While the possession of just these rights is community specific, our grounds for prizing rights and rights communities is not specific to our or any other one community, although it is specific to the history that has shaped our own and other communities as distinctively modern ones. While rights can only be enjoyed within a community, the goodness of the idea of a rights community itself and the moral basis for communal membership are not themselves communally specific. Hence we cannot believe that having the rights we do is morally good without believing that all others ought also to be right holders.

If having rights requires belonging to a rights community and we believe all others ought to be able to belong to such a community, then we enact our belief in (human) rights by attempting to transform existing states that are not rights-based into rights-based communities. Or, if we judge that the end of having individuals belong to a rights based community can be achieved more effectively this way, we support the demands of groups that they be recognized as autonomous (democratic and rights-) based states. The choice between these two options, which seems so pertinent and difficult at present, is itself practical and not moral. In pursing the first option we use all the resources available: documenting, shaming, publicizing, employing sanctions, and so forth. To the degree with which we really regard all nation states as sovereign, these strategies, while important, are limited in their potential effectiveness. But, in fact, if we believe that human communities are only choice-worthy if they are rights respecting, then we might well believe that sovereignty ought to be limited. While there may be insuperable practical difficulties in acting on this belief, it says no more than that we have no moral obligation to recognize the unlimited sovereignty of a nation state that does not itself recognize the moral claim of its citizens to be rights holders. This moral restriction on sovereignty is no different in kind than the restriction that makes genocide, for example, a disqualification of sovereignty.

Given the practical difficulties in acting on this belief, we have come up with an interesting partial solution. As a condition for our community recognizing the legitimacy of other communities we ask those other communities to make themselves signatories to declarations whereby they commit themselves to act on those rights we regard as the minimum necessary for a rights community. Simultaneously, we set up bodies, above all supra-commmunal judiciaries, that are courts of appeal against state law. In pursuing this strategy we are doing two things. First we are widening the potential rights community beyond the boundaries of actual states, and secondly, we are providing the claim of rights against mere legality with legal machinery that is itself not state-based. That we should pursue such a strategy is itself rationally consistent with the view of rights being espoused here since it tacitly acknowledges that there is an ultimate contingency in the fact that the world is populated by just the states and communities it is, and further that it is a matter of moral luck that we, and those in a position like ours, are members of rights-based and rights-respecting communities.

Neither contingency nor moral luck (a kind of contingency) are fully rationalizable. Nonetheless, this strategy reworks, at the level of communities themselves, the logic of transition from the implicit and potential to explicit and actual that represented the movement into rights for individuals and groups within communities. The justification for believing that this logic is applicable to communities themselves is the overdetermined recognition — derived from the logic of communal membership, the contingency of our communal membership and the contingency of there being just the communities there are — that communities are logically porous at the reflective level. Here this means, no community will count for us as a rationally self-determining community unless it is, at least, implicitly and potentially a rights community. So the only logic through which we might recognise any community as independent and self-determining puts it into relation with other such communities.

Once we take on board the logic of potentiality, we are forced to recognize that the distinction between manifesto rights and actual rights is not itself absolute. Rights are always a matter of degree. But if this is so then the practice of rights, the effort of documenting rights violations, publicising our findings, measuring the degree to which different states recognize rights and so forth, are significant parts of a practice that makes the so-called rights we believe people are morally entitled to, actual. And that matters.

WHAT THE AGENDA HAS BEEN MISSING

JAMES D SEYMOUR

I HAVE BEEN ASKED TO CONVEY to you the view from west of the Atlantic regarding the Chinese democracy movement. At first I despaired at this, not being sure that there is an American or North American view regarding the question of Chinese democracy. However, after considerable reflection I think there are some meaningful observations that can be made. This is a subject that was quite sensitive a decade ago but it no longer is. Once those of us who cared about the issue of human rights were told by our sinologist colleagues that we were trying to apply to China values which are parochial and inapplicable. Now only a tiny minority of those interested in China hold this view and the issue is no longer whether China needs democracy, but rather what kind of democracy is appropriate. On this question the main cleavage is between recent arrivals from China and the remainder of us.

The answer to the question posed by this conference depends on one's conception of the purpose of human rights. If one sees them as ends in themselves, then all we need to consider are the practical means of attaining them in China. However, most Chinese seem to think of rights as instrumental. While this may not be wrong, I worry when people think of rights as merely a means to an end: it suggests that rights can be disregarded whenever a case can be made that human rights observance would not serve the needs of public policy. Indeed, that is the official Chinese view: human rights are all well and good, but the public interest requires their suspension. The official media often contains articles about human rights.[1] The authorities want this issue ventilated because they know it is a powerful one, and they do not wish the discussion to be dominated by their opponents.

---

[1] The most authoritative statement of the Chinese position is contained in the State Council's so-called White Paper, 'Human Rights in China', an English translation of which appeared in both *Beijing Review*, November 4, 1991, pp. 8–45 and in U.S. Foreign Broadcast Information Service, *Daily Report: China* (hereafter: FBIS), supplement, November 21, 1991, pp. 1–29.

Even the Chinese public appears to accept the view that the value of human rights lies in their instrumentality. As a writer of the Democracy Wall era put it: 'For the average citizen, the purpose of demanding democracy and rights is to promote national construction and prosperity for the whole nation. There should be no other purposes.'[1]

This is quite different from the American view that human rights have a sacred quality: inasmuch as they are seen as inherent, it is almost a sacrilege to ask whether they are useful.

Still, we believe that they *are* useful. More to the point: *democracy* is useful, and human rights are a precondition of democracy. After all, without the free flow of ideas and information, government cannot be held accountable to the people, which is the essence of democracy. China's authorities constantly complain about corruption and other malpractices, but claim that the 'instruments of dictatorship' can adequately deal with the problem.[2] Actually, under this approach things have simply gone from bad to worse. Only if people have the freedom to take political action against errant officials can the problem of corruption be brought under control. What is needed is *liberal* democracy.

Some would say that the term 'liberal democracy' is tautologous. While I am inclined to agree, I think we have to address seriously the idea that there is also such a thing as 'non-liberal democracy'. He Baogang has given a thoughtful argument for this, namely that Chinese paternalism deserves to be considered a variant of democracy (though he agrees that it is far from ideal).[3] The reason I want to address this issue here is because most Chinese intellectuals, especially the so-called 'upper-echelon intellectuals' (*gaoji zhishifenzi*), seem to favour a kind of paternalistic democracy. While it would be going too far to say that the kind of democracy they advocate is indistinguishable from the fake democracy heralded by China's leaders, there is a worrisome similarity. Despite its disastrous history, the idea that China will be saved by China's intellectuals dies hard and there is little recognition of what a tiny social stratum they comprise. Any system that

[1] 'Realizing the Four Modernizations: Democratic National Construction, and the Contending of the Hundred Schools', *Democracy and Modernity* (minzhu yu shidai), no. 1, translated in James D. Seymour, ed., *The Fifth Modernization: China's Human Rights Movement, 1978–1979*, (Coleman, Stanfordville, N.Y. 1980), p. 35.

[2] For example, see Procurator General Liu Fuzhi's speech to procurators, New China News Agency (NCNA), May 24, 1991, FBIS, CHI–91–102, pp. 41 f., and that of the director of the State Council's office for correcting departmental malpractice, NCNA, May 24, 1991, ibid., p. 42.

[3] He Baogang, 'A Critique of the Chinese Paternalistic Model of Democracy', *Issues and Studies*, vol. 26 no. 10 (October 1990), pp. 24–42.

relies heavily on them is going to be paternalistic at best, and it will probably be elitist and unaccountable to the people. This may be 'democracy' (whether it is or not is largely a matter of semantics), but it is not the kind of *liberal* democracy promised in the documents collectively known as the Universal Bill of Human Rights.[1] It is also not the kind of democracy that will lead to social development and political modernization. For these, one needs liberal democracy, i.e., democracy based on human rights in the broadest sense. The entire population must be encouraged to participate in the political process, and leaders and aspiring leaders must have a sense of accountability to the general public.

In a democracy, leaders are public servants and should not be taken too seriously. To quote the gadfly political philosopher Liu Xiaobo: 'Why do the Chinese constantly re-enact the same tragedy (one starting with Qu Yuan's drowning in the Miluo River)? Why do the Chinese mourn as tragic heros people like Zhou Enlai, Peng Dehuai, and Hu Yaobang, while they forget such tragic figures as Wei Jingsheng?'[2] It is interesting that Liu resonates primarily with the humble electrician Wei, who was the first to argue for a 'fifth modernization' (democracy). China needs more non-leaders like him. But, says Liu, 'The Chinese love to look up to the famous, thereby saving themselves the trouble of thinking; that is why the Chinese rush into things en masse.'[3] Actually, this is at least as true of Americans as it is of Chinese (I am not certain about Britons!), but we have institutional safeguards to limit the damage that misguided leaders can inflict. Anyway, Liu is certainly on the right track when he castigates his countrymen for their fawning admiration of people like Hu Yaobang and Zhou Enlai (as though such men, had they only been given a free hand in China's problems, would have solved them). Liu sees such leaders in quite a different light, but (more to the point) argues that it is a mistake to focus on any *leader*; what is needed is not better leaders but empowered followers.

Chinese intellectuals therefore are quite right in giving primacy to the question of civil liberties, but if they talk only of this and of wresting power

[1] This term embraces the Universal Declaration of Human Rights (proclaimed 1948), the International Covenant on Economic, Social and Cultural Rights (entered into force in 1976), and the International Covenant on Civil and Political Rights (entered into force 1976).

[2] Geremie Barmé, 'Confession, Redemption, and Death: Liu Xiaobo and the Protest Movement of 1989', in George Hicks, ed., *The Broken Mirror: China After Tiananmen*, (St. James Press, Chicago 1990), p. 61.

[3] *'Weiji'*, *Shenzhen qingnianbao*, October 3, 1986, quoted in Barmé, ibid. p. 53.

from the Communists, there is a question of sincerity.[1] Furthermore, they will give credence to the Party's charges about 'bourgeois humanism'. Intellectuals are not apt to gain much headway if they allow the communists to monopolize the issues of the rights — at least the economic ones — of workers and farmers. Communists, after all, claim to be the vanguard of the working class, which, in its turn, is said to be the leading segment of society. While I personally do not subscribe to the view that 'economic rights' are 'human rights' in the same sense that civil liberties are,[2] I take very seriously Article 21 of the UN's Universal Declaration of Human Rights, which says that 'The will of the people shall be the basis of the authority of government', and that 'everyone has the right to take part in the government' through 'free voting procedures'.

'Everyone' must mean *everyone*. In general, China's intellectuals have shown little sympathy for the notion that democracy means rule of the majority; Liu Xiaobo is the main exception that comes to mind. Although Liu is indeed a critic of China's political system and leaders, he is best known for his scathing indictments of the establishment intellectuals, including many who are usually considered democrats. Liu insists that they are not democrats, because democracy requires that people behave democratically. His advice to the Tiananmen demonstrators was to show that *they* do things differently — that they could conduct their movement by democratic means — and, therefore that the students *and workers* should each hold democratic elections to choose their leaders. He wanted to see Poland's Solidarity phenomenon replicated in China, but with farmers (as well as urban workers) leading the campaign for political change and democratisation so that, ultimately, each sector of the populace would be organized in a way that would enable them to represent their interests in

[1] Some luminaries of the Federation for a Democratic China were in Zhao Ziyang's camp, and were he to be rehabilitated they might return to the government. Both the FDC and the Chinese Alliance for Democracy have accepted funds from the Kuomintang. This has been especially blatant in the case of the FDC. As two journalists have written, 'it is a simple switch from one Leninist party to another.' Stacy Mosher and Lincoln Kay, 'Home Thoughts Abroad: Chinese Dissidents in US grope for post-Tiananmen Role', *Far Eastern Economic Review*, June 6, 1991, p. 35.

[2] For the purposes of this paper, 'human rights' refers primarily to civil liberties. Although economic and cultural rights have been declared 'human' rights, in reality they are citizenship rights, i.e. rights which one has because a government chooses to grant them, not because one is a member of the human race. In other words, one has economic rights by virtue of one's membership in a polity which recognizes such rights. When governments deny civil liberties, on the other hand, they are violating 'international' norms, and humans (as distinct from citizens) have at least a theoretical claim against the international community for rescue if not redress. No such claim, even theoretically, exists in the case of economic rights.

the political process. It is not surprising that the Communists put Liu Xiaobo in prison, but one is taken aback by the lack of support his suggestions generated among the 'upper echelon intellectuals'.[1]

Perhaps I am being presumptuous, but I think that if there is a 'North American' view of these matters, it lies closer to Liu Xiaobo than to his numerous critics. It is this issue, the question of the extent to which democracy should be broad-based, that divides many North Americans (I cannot speak for other Westerners or Japanese) from Chinese intellectuals. Of course, by 'North Americans' I mean people who have been in the United States or Canada[2] for more than a few years, which includes many people of Chinese descent.

I distinguish such people from the recent arrivals from China. The latter tend towards such well-known international Chinese organizations as:–

CAD: Chinese Alliance for Democracy (*Minlian*). Founded in 1982–83. (The other organizations on this list were founded around 1989.) Publishes *China Spring* (in Chinese).

FDC: Federation for a Democratic China (*Minzhen*). Based in Paris, with national branches (*zhibu*) elsewhere.

IFCSS: International Federation of Chinese Scholars and Students (*Xuelian*). Interested in the education of students and the research of Chinese scholars in the US, as well as promoting Chinese democracy. Less political than the above, though the organization does lobby the US government.

What is interesting about these associations is their lack of appeal, especially among those who are not recent arrivals from China. This is in part because of the infighting among their heads and the malfeasance of certain leaders. But more important, I suspect, is the elitist notions that the leaders of these organizations have about 'democracy'.

At any rate, I find many people gravitating toward another type of association, namely, Community Based Organizations (CBOs, or *shequ minlian zuzhi*). The major such coalition, at least in the Western hemisphere, is the North American Coalition for Chinese Democracy (NACCD), composed

---

[1] There are many reasons why Liu antagonizes his fellow-intellectuals, and this may not be one of the important ones. On Liu, see Barmé op. cit. pp. 52–99.
[2] The author apologises for omitting Mexico from this discussion.

of five organizations.[1] In addition, there are numerous local organizations in the United States and Canada which co-operate with NACCD bodies. Normally, the local organizations work only with their localities to promote the cause of Chinese democracy but there is, much 'networking' by means of fax, email, telephone, etc. Only infrequently is there real collaboration and on rare occasions coalition members hold joint conferences.

Although it is hazardous to generalise, it seems to me that two things distinguish CBOs from the mainline organizations. First, members of CBOs eschew centralized societies in the belief that democracy must be 'bottom-up' rather than 'top-down'. They are also alienated from the mainstream organizations, especially FDC, which they consider inefficient, and largely concerned with leadership struggles.[2] The CBOs have no international (or even national) headquarters, but simply form coalitions.

The second difference has to do with social and economic issues. Here I must digress for a moment. In the West, employers have limited authority over employees. If a person is fired, it is bad but it is not the end of the world. One probably does not lose one's home, and usually there is some provision for health-care and other basic needs. In China these are usually functions of the work unit (*danwei*) and there is also less job mobility than in the West so that if one loses one's job one loses everything. The threat of unemployment is a major change from the Mao era, and has presented the regime with an unprecedented legitimacy crisis. As Wang Shaoguang has noted:

> Were one to single out one factor conditioning workers' support for communist regimes, it would be an expectation of protection from insecurity, inequality, and uncertainty by a strong welfare state. Deng Xiaoping gambled on being able to compensate Chinese workers with greater prosperity in exchange for any erosion of security, equality and certainty ... The gamble failed.[3]

[1] The NACCD's full members are: Federation of Overseas Hong Kong Chinese (Washington), Foundation for Chinese Democracy (San Francisco), South Californian Foundation for Chinese Democracy (Los Angeles), Tiananmen Memorial Foundation (New York/New Jersey), Toronto Association for Democracy in China, and the Vancouver Society in Support of the Democratic Movement.
[2] This has certainly been so in the past. However, it has become less true of CAD in recent years, and now even the FDC is improving.
[3] Wang Shaoguang, 'The Role of Chinese Workers', in Jia Hao, ed., *The Democracy Movement of 1989 and China's Future*, (The Washington Center for Chinese Studies, Washington 1990), p. 99.

Deng Xiaoping's industrial reforms in fact gave plant managers more power than ever over workers. leading to a situation whereby workers need to satisfy the manager, or not only be without a job but also without a home, health care, etc. The result is constant tension between employer and employee, which at best results in passive resistance. Sometimes there are fights and even murders.

Of course, some of the workers' grievances have been simply economic. Adjusted for inflation, real wages have grown little. Workers have watched while the standard of living of the corrupt and powerful (as well as the clever) has risen greatly, while that of those who produce the goods has not. Perhaps if the regime had somehow managed to raise their standard of living, the workers could have been silenced. This had happened in the case of the peasants, who had been bought off by Deng's land reforms. Not only did peasant income triple,[1] but the reforms gave the majority of farmers a degree of autonomy and control over their lives that is not even in sight for urban workers.

What would 'industrial democracy' mean in the context of the Chinese workplace? Here we must distinguish between the socialist and private sectors. In state enterprises there is already considerable security and freedom at the shop level. Even though workers have little input on the larger business questions,[2] it has not been easy for even China's conservative reformers to convince workers that there would be anything in economic reform for them. The line for democrats should be that the proper way to offset the short-run risks of inflation and job security is political empowerment, and that with this workers hitherto employed by the state will be able to enjoy the fruits of the reformed, more productive economy. While that is probably true, were I a Chinese state sector worker I would be difficult to convince.

But the state sector is dying and private enterprise is the way of the future. And here lies the real opportunity for Chinese democrats. Working conditions in private enterprise are atrocious.[3] Today, even impoverished workers in the Philippines cannot compete with the exploited Chinese workers in the special economic zones. Capitalism is simply not a humane

---

[1] *Christian Science Monitor*, October 19, 1990, p. 1.

[2] Little has changed since October 6, 1980, when *Workers Daily* admitted that working people often 'have little to say about important issues in theory enterprises.'

[3] Leung Wing-Yue, *Smashing the Iron Rice Pot: Workers and Unions in China's Market Socialism* (Asia Monitor Resource Centre, Hong Kong 1988). Anita Chan's review of this book (with extensive excerpts) appeared in *China Information* (Spring 1991) pp. 75–80.

system unless the state government guarantees the workers' right to organize and unless it provides a welfare safety-net for those who cannot survive in the labour market. Chinese democrats must seize upon this issue, and present a platform that combines civil liberties with workers' rights. That is the only way to win workers away from the so-called party of the proletariat (a point on which the Party still insists[1]); the communists will remain in power until the public — 'the broad masses' — is offered a better alternative.

Unions, of course, will be the key and there are two possible ways that workers may come to be provided with independent and therefore helpful trade unions. The first would be for the existing trade union apparatus to break away from the Communist Party and really become a workers' organization. One might laugh at that prospect, inasmuch as these unions' functions and workers' interests seem to have been at cross-purposes. This, however, is not the whole story. It will be recalled that the unions were disbanded in 1967, charged with 'economism' or being too concerned with workers' needs. But in the 1980s the Trade Union Federation tended to take a neutral stance on the question of workers' going on strike — neither encouraging nor forbidding the practice. Furthermore, in the spring of 1989 the Federation, in a remarkable demonstration of independence, donated 100,000 *yuan* to the Tiananmen demonstrators (the only official agency to give them financial support). Then the Federation's executive committee reportedly voted to call a nationwide general strike.[2] However, Federation head Zhu Houze hesitated and meanwhile Li Peng declared martial law. The incident suggests the possibility of the union structure detaching itself from Party control, which would be the first step toward serving the interests of the working class and — more importantly for our purposes today — giving workers an avenue for participating in the political life of the country.

---

[1] In recent years some Chinese have promoted the notion that the Communist Party should be the party of all the people, not just urban workers. This idea has now been authoritatively rejected. In May, Song Ping reiterated: 'The [industrial] working class represents advanced production forces. It is the most selfless, most revolutionary, and most advanced, and it best represents the fundamental interests of all people ... Our socialist undertakings must be led by the working class and its political party, the CCP. The advocacy of the so-called all-people party has obscured the Party's class nature and advancement, and had denied the working class's and the Communist Party's leadership. It actually is aimed at changing the Party's nature, so it runs counter to the fundamental interests of the broad masses.' Beijing television, May 29, 1991, FBIS CHI-91-105, p. 14 f.

[2] This information was given to me by a usually reliable source.

THE CONCEPT OF RIGHTS

The alternative would be for the emergence of entirely new autonomous unions. Indeed, some of these were established in the spring of 1989. Mindful of what happened in Poland, the authorities found these a much greater threat to their power and privilege than they found the student demonstrators. They started arresting workers *before* June 4th, and after that date most of the arrests and all of the executions were of workers.[1] The leader of the independent union in Shanghai, the most industrialized city, was shown on television being held at gunpoint, his face badly swollen, apparently from beatings. Arrests of union organizers were still taking place in 1991.[2] All this should not surprise us. The Communists had always considered the workers the most politically advanced class and the backbone of their movement — a myth that had been crucial to the Party's legitimacy. In 1991 they claimed to be taking steps 'to widen the channels through which workers may participate in political affairs, so as to make the workers really feel that they are masters of the state and of their enterprises.'[3] In this respect, surely democrats can offer the workers more than do the Communists.

In some respects, the 1989 demonstrations marked a major stride toward the achievement of 'civil society' which political scientists tell us democracy requires. One worries, however, about how urban-centred it was. In this respect, the Tiananmen demonstrations mark a retrogression from the 1978–79 'democracy wall' movement centred one or two kilometres to the west at Xidan. Those earlier democrats thought of themselves as *gongmin*,

[1] Among arrested workers are: Cao Zihui, Cheng Hongli, Cao Yingyun, Guo Yaxiong, Han Dongfang, He Qunyin, Li Jiang, Li Mingxian, Li Mou, Li Zixi, Liang Qiang, Liang Zhenyun, Liu Huanwen, Liu Qiang, Sun Feng, Sun Hong, Sun Jizhong, Sun Yanru, Tang Minglu, Tian Bomin, Wang Lianxi, Wu Qiang, Yan Fuqian, Yang Fuqiang, Yi Jinyao, You Dianqi, Yu Peiming, Yu Tieliang, Zhang Jianzhong, Zhang Shu, Zhou Endong, Zhou Shaowu and Zhu Lianyi. (Some of these have been released) [Ed. *June 4 China Support* produces a complete list of known arrests twice a year with biographical and arrest details where available. For a copy contact J4CS. Similar information is provided by Amnesty International and Asia Watch. Most arrests are not reported and the true number can only therefore be guessed: Asia Watch's document *Anthems of Defeat: Crackdown in Hunan Province 1989–1991* (Asia Watch, New York and Washington 1992) listing over 200 imprisoned workers in one province gives an idea of the scale of the arrests.]
[2] Li Lin, a leader of the Workers' Autonomous Association in Hunan, was reportedly arrested in 1991, along with his brother Li Zhi, *South China Morning Post*, June 1, 1991, p. 1, FBIS CHI-91-106, p. 31. [Ed. See also Asia Watch report, ibid.]
[3] Quan Shuren, 'Strengthen and Improve the Party's Work Toward the Working Class Under the New Historical Conditions', *Qiushi*, May 1, 1991, pp. 9–13, FBIS CHI-91-111, p. 34.

44

whereas in 1989 the byword was *shimin*.[1] While both terms can be translated 'citizen', *shimin* literally means 'citizen' in the old Anglo-French sense of the word: city dweller. China has not made the same linguistic progress that the English-speaking people have, but it is not merely a matter of semantics. Indeed, all of this is historically correct, for rural types were little in evidence in 1989.[2] This was the major failing of Tiananmen.

Let us think back for a minute. The Communists rode to power on the promise of land for the peasants. Their failure to keep that promise brought many peasants into the democracy movement of 1978–79. In part because of that warning, the Communists undertook to keep to the earlier promise and now seem to have most of the farmers (who comprise at least two-thirds of the population) in their camp. This class, and the peasant–based army, are the real political basis of their dictatorship and democrats neglect this fact at their peril.

Since farmers now have their land, are there any issues left on which democrats can make an appeal to them? I think there are. In the first place, commoditization of agricultural products has created serious economic stratification in the countryside. Indeed, there are now 100 million surplus rural workers. They are pouring into cities, 80,000 arriving a day in Guangzhou alone. The authorities' response to the resulting social problems is callous. 'We should promptly send back rovers...' Deputy Party Secretary Ni Hongfu has said.[3] There is an urgent need for legal and welfare state protection for the impoverished.

But more fundamentally, the farmers need political empowerment. This idea causes most Chinese intellectuals to wince: 'What do ignorant peasants know about politics?' Well, my answer to that is that if peasants are smart enough to feed intellectuals then they are smart enough to make some input into the political process. To be sure, education will be needed, but always before, we have been told, a period of 'tutelage' must precede political empowerment. This is a fallacy. The farmers can learn politics the same way other people do: by doing. Indeed, the communists have been

[1] See, for example, the famous 'Letter to President Carter', which was signed 'Gongmin'. Text translated in Seymour, op. cit. pp. 227–239.
[2] Farmers were not completely absent from the 1989 demonstrations. Zhang Boli (one of the '21 Most Wanted Students', an escapee from China) told me that Tiananmen demonstrators received about 500 telegrams from villages around the country, and that an Inner Mongolian herdsman came all the way to the capital on horseback to show his support. Aside from Beijing, there were agrarian demonstrations in Nanjing, certain smaller cities, and in such rural areas as Anhui Province.
[3] Sydney [Australia] *Morning Herald*, June 15, 1991.

taking steps to effect greater involvement in village politics.[1] However, when it comes to *national* politics, the communists show no signs of wanting to share power with anyone, least of all the farmers. The rural populace is seriously under-represented in the People's Congresses, and because of the over-representation of cities at various levels in the congresses, a rural delegate to the National People's Congress (NPC) represents roughly eleven times as many people as do urban delegates.[2] This hardly matters because the NPC has no power anyway, but rural under-representation is one of the things that must be changed before China can be deemed democratic.

In 1992 a scholar from China gave a talk at Columbia University in which he proclaimed himself in favour of democracy but urged foreigners not to apply pressure on the Chinese government to liberalize. Sceptical, I asked the man what he meant by democracy. He explained that he meant more freedom for the intellectuals. 'What' I asked, 'about all the other people?' He replied, that one must understand that most Chinese are peasants who would vote according to misperceived parochial interests not the national welfare, and so must be kept out of politics. He would not even address the issue of political participation by urban workers.

This notion — that democracy (in the Chinese context) means substitution of one group of autocrats for the incumbents — is the most disturbing aspect of China's democracy movement. Of course, there are notable exceptions, but the number of Chinese reformers and dissidents concerned with empowering the majority is very small. Both the reformers and the dissidents are essentially urban in their orientation. While the idea of placing political power in the hands of farmers strikes most Chinese intellectuals as ludicrous, it seems quite natural to a North American. After all, we started out as an *agrarian* democracy: the US war of independence was led by farmers who then set up a political system. The political order they created was far from perfect but it demonstrated that farmers can play politics just as well as anyone else. China's experience of the last few hundred years hardly proves that intellectuals are the best ones to run things. Time and time again the state has been placed in their hands and each time they have failed. Of course, they will have an important role to

---

[1] See, for example, Yan Zhenguo and Su Huihai, 'Beijing Municipality's Tongxian County has Explored a New Way to Promote Grass-roots Democracy by Instituting the System of Keeping the Public Informed of Administrative Affairs', NCNA, May 11, 1991, FBIS CHI–91–093, p. 69.

[2] Officially the ratio is 8:1. See J. Bruce Jacobs, 'Elections in China', *Australian Journal of Chinese Affairs*, no. 25 (January 1991), p. 177.

play in China's future, but they will only be constructive if they work with all groups in society. After all, whoever runs the country must be accountable to the general public, or the result will simply be not-so-new authoritarianism.

In this connection, there is one Chinese notion that strikes many of us as odd. Ever since 1919 we have been told that 'Mr Democracy' goes hand-in-hand with 'Mr Science'. But the world has experienced too many rights-denying technocracies (including post-Mao China[1]) to give that notion much credence. Science, after all, is the quest for truth or at least relative truth. Democracy has little to do with truth: rather, it is about values and about 'who gets what'. China's intellectuals are strong on the idea of national plans drawn up by specialists. On the other hand, these 'scientists' (especially social scientists) want freedom from political interference.[2] Actually science, which is largely financed by the public, must be accountable to the public, which means either the marketplace or the government has a legitimate role to play. One still wants the scientific community to have considerable autonomy so that all the weaknesses of proposed state policies can be fully exposed. The point is that there is bound to be much tension between 'Mr Science' and 'Mr Democracy'. On questions of the uses to which science and technology are to be put, non-scientist citizens must have the final say.[3]

Chinese intellectuals will have to get over the idea that they will save China: they will not. If it is to be saved at all it will be by a broad coalition of which the intellectuals will be a tiny minority. They need to learn to talk less and listen more.

There are two other matters that (in the parlance of this conference's theme) ought to 'happen next'. First we must increase the pressure on the Taiwanese authorities to begin respecting human rights and to allow the

[1] See Li Cheng and Lynn White, 'Elite Transformation and Modern Change in Mainland China and Taiwan: Empirical Data and the Theory of Technocracy', *China Quarterly*, vol. 121 (March 1990), pp. 1–35, and — 'The Thirteenth Central Committee of the Chinese Communist Party: From Mobilizers to Managers', *Asian Survey*, vol. 25 no. 4 (April 1988), pp. 371–99.
[2] Note, for example, Yan Jiaqi's 'three nos' for science: no forbidden zones, no idols, and no pinnacles (i.e. no consummate theories). *Yan Jiaqi and China's Struggle for Democracy*, (M E Sharpe, London 1991, pp. 36 f.
[3] The science-democracy relationship in the Chinese context will be addressed by Lynn White in an article 'Mr Science vs. Mr Democracy?', being prepared for a book edited by Cao Tianyu. See also Christopher Buckley, 'Science as Politics and Politics as Science: Fang Lizhi and Chinese Intellectuals' Uncertain Road to Dissent', *Australian Journal of Chinese Affairs*, no. 25 (January 1991), pp. 1–36.

island to become a democracy. Whether or not Taiwan is ever integrated into China, it might still stand as an inspiration to people on the other side of the straits. However, before that happens the Guomintang must be compelled to release its critics from prison and to allow a government to come into being based on informed free choice and 'one-person one-vote' as expressed in fair elections. Much recent propaganda to the contrary notwithstanding, Taiwan has a long way to go in these respects.[1] If the island's rulers can be persuaded to change their ways, this would be a major contribution to the democratization of China.

The second issue concerns Tibet. The Tibet question is a good litmus test to determine whether a Chinese is an independent thinker and a real supporter of human rights. If people insist on believing the Communist's disinformation campaign regarding the history of Tibet then they are more nationalists than democrats. Very few Chinese intellectuals pass this test. One who does, Su Xiaokang, observed at the January 1991 conference in New York, 'It is as if when we hear a Tibetan has been killed, we don't really think that it is a human life that has been lost.' Some democracy movement leaders (such as Zhang Boli) take the view that Sino-American trade should be contingent on improved human rights for Han Chinese, but should not be tied to improvements in Tibet's human rights situation. The Tibetans have a right to self-determination and anyone who would deny them that and yet insist on freedom for himself is being hypocritical.

To conclude, one answer to the title question of this conference 'Rights in China: What Happens Next?' is that we need to integrate our thinking about human rights with a transcendent framework for democracy. There is a broad consensus both abroad and among people in China on the subject of civil liberties, after all, no one enjoys being pushed around by arbitrary cadres and hardly anyone outside the government believes it is appropriate to imprison people because of their beliefs. In the absence of democracy, respect for human rights may not advance a society much. *We* know that, but how many people in China know that? We must focus on the problem of making the idea of democracy appealing to the *lao bai xing*: China's labouring classes must be made to realize that there is something in it for them; the farmers must be persuaded to think of decollectivization as the beginning, and not the end, of social development; and the myth of the proletarian state must be exploded for the urban workers— they must be promised, and granted, democracy in the workplace. But China's intellectuals will have a tough job convincing them that they will be better

[1] In 1992 almost all Taiwanese political prisoners were released.

off under capitalism than under socialism. Indeed it is probably not true *unless* capitalism is accompanied by worker empowerment, and this should therefore be a high priority on the agenda of Chinese democrats.

DEMOCRACY AS A SAFEGUARD FOR BASIC HUMAN RIGHTS

CHAN HONG-MO ET AL.
Alliance for a Better China[1]

MY TASK IS A RELATIVELY SIMPLE ONE. I have been asked to give a short report on a small research project initiated by the *Alliance for a Better China*, of which I am a member. The first results of the project have been published in the Alliance's magazine, *Forum for a Better China*.[2]

I should first explain that the *Alliance* is a voluntary international group, consisting mainly of professionals of Chinese origin, formed soon after the tragic events of June 4th 1989. Its aims are to promote human rights and democracy in China, and its *Forum* magazine, which is distributed world-wide, is intended to be a vehicle for achieving those aims.

There are two approaches one can take in tackling the problem of human rights in a country like China. One way is to identify specific cases of human right violations and then to mobilize world opinion so as to try to force their removal. Such a tactic is pursued vigorously by, for example, Amnesty International, and we have good reason to believe that it has been effective in securing relatively light sentences in trials of Chinese dissidents and in improving their treatment in custody.[3] Another approach, which is more difficult but equally essential in the long term, is to work towards fostering respect for human rights in the country targeted. In view of the composition of our membership, the *Alliance* feels that it is particularly suited for this second task as regards China.

---

[1] This paper was presented at the conference by Chan Hong-Mo on behalf of the *Alliance for a Better China*. The authors of the paper are: Chan Hong-Mo (theoretical physicist), Chan Man-Suen (biologist), Mo Joe-Nin (experimental physicist), Ali Namazie (theoretical physicist), Tsou Sheung Tsun (mathematician), Joseph T. Y. Wong (virologist) and Chan Man-Kwun (social and political scientist).

[2] *Forum for a Better China*, no. 2, (English edition summer 1991, Chinese edition autumn 1991). Copies of the magazine are available by post from the following address: Forum Sales, Alliance for a Better China, PO Box 59, Didcot, Oxon OX11 OQZ, UK.

[3] I am referring here to the trials which took place in late 1990/early 1991. See Amnesty International's various reports, especially ASA 17/020/91 *People's Republic of China: Trials of dissidents, sentences and releases in Beijing* (1st February, 1991).

There is no doubt a cultural aspect to the problem, but at least in the case of China, I personally believe that this has often been overstated. Although differing in details, human rights are basically universal. Having been brought up in China but living most of my professional life in the West, I have had the chance to observe both cultures at close range and noted the fundamental similarity. In the simplest terms, we, as human beings all love life and abhor the destruction of it. If Chinese culture did not also have this it would not have survived for four thousand years. What happened at Tiananmen in June 1989 violated all human values and was inexcusable in whatever cultural background. Rather, I believe that much of the cause is in the political system. In a discussion two days ago in Oxford with Dr Anthony Grayling, who is present in the audience, he remarked that governments never act for reasons of morality, only expediency. I fully endorse this. The Chinese government, when it felt itself threatened, behaved as it did because the political system allowed it to do so. On the other hand, a government in a democracy will be far less ready to resort to brutality. It is not so much that an elected government is necessarily morally superior, but that it is mechanically constrained simply by the knowledge that it is in some way answerable for its actions and in the next round of elections it may be voted out.

Though seemingly obvious to those used to living under a democratic system, these views are apparently not shared by all Chinese nationals. Indeed, in a communication to the *Forum*, a recent emigre from China declared: 'What I want for China is just basic human rights if we have that, I do not care whether the country is a democracy or a dictatorship'. On other words, not being used to how a democratic system works, he was sceptical that there was any correlation between democracy and human rights. Now, being mostly natural scientists by profession, our members reacted to such a confrontation in a typical, perhaps oversimplistic, manner. Whether such a correlation exists is merely a matter of facts, and most of us being professional adepts at dallying with facts, we set ourselves the task to find out — hence the project on which I now wish to report.

The purpose of the project then is to clarify the relationship, if any, between the human rights record of a country and the level of democracy in its government. The aim is to analyse the existing data in an as objective and quantitative manner as possible. The hope is that such an analysis will help answer the question whether democracy is indeed useful as a safeguard for human rights. We should stress that it is not out intention to examine the human rights or democracy records of any particular country; the data will be analysed entirely in a statistical manner without mentioning countries by name.

To perform such an analysis, the first thing we need is a scoring system to gauge the 'level of democracy' of any government. By democracy we mean here simply the right of the people to decide on the manner a country is governed. The object of a scoring system is to grade the nations of the world according to the degree they allow their people to exercise that right. We wish to do so without being biased by other factors, such as whether the countries adopt a capitalist or socialist economic system, so as to make any correlation found between human rights and democracy as unambiguous as possible. We want a sufficiently clear-cut set of criteria which, once specified, will lead we hope to the same score independently of the scorer, given the same data. Also the criteria should not be so hard to satisfy as to exclude most countries, and should ideally be such as to give an even distribution of the world's nations over the different grades.

After some thought, we arrived at a scoring system in which we give the scorer a score sheet comprising seven questions. The scorer is asked to apply each of these questions to each country in turn and, on the basis of the answer to the question, award the country a mark (a number between 0 and 1). The sum total of the marks for all seven questions is the final democracy score D for that country. The higher the total score D of a country, the more democratic is deemed to be its government. The lowest score possible is 0 and the highest is 7. The countries are divided into eight grades on the basis of these scores, the zeroth with $D=0$, the first with $0<D<1$, the second with $1<D<2$, and so on.

I shall not give any detail here of the actual questions posed except to say that they were quite complex and took account of both the country's existing political system, and of its political history over the past fifteen years, and how effectively its democratic system had functioned over this period. We recognize that our scoring system is far from perfect. The mere question of what actually constitutes democracy is a profound sociological one on which an expert could easily spend a whole lifetime. We are not so naive as to think that we, being mostly inexperienced in the subject, have hit upon a superior system for gauging democracy in general. We believe, however — and as we shall see, the results of our analysis supports this belief — that correlations between human rights and democracy are 'first order effects' which can already be seen even with such a crude system of gauging democracy as ours. In a similar fashion, although a cup of water is made up of billions upon billions of atoms, each of which will take a natural scientist a lifetime to start to understand, we would not require this detailed knowledge to be convinced that water is non-poisonous and thirst-quenching.

Our scoring system for democracy was applied to all 164 independent states existing in the world in 1989, using data complied in Chamber's *Political Systems of the World*[1], leading to a score D for each country. In principle, with this score for democracy, one can immediately compare it with any scoring system for human right's record and look for correlations.

Chamber's compilation also gives a human rights rating for 87 or the countries listed. It is given in the form of a percentage, the higher the percentage, then the better its human rights record. These data are entered together with the above score D into the scatter plot shown in Fig. 1. For each of the 87 countries with a human rights rating, say R, we enter a point with R as the ordinate and D as the abscissa. The result is Fig. 1 where a positive correlation between R and D can be clearly seen. For readers who are not familiar with scatter plots, we have also presented the average human rights rating R for each of the eight democracy grades (Fig. 2). Again, one notices that the human rights rating is high when the democracy grade is high, meaning that on average, more democratic countries tend to have better human rights records.

Although the correlation noted above is quite unambiguous, we are unsure about two points. First, the manner in which the human rights rating R was derived and, secondly, the fact that R was given for only about half the countries which might lead to bias. We therefore sought an independent check. We took the annual reports of Amnesty International for the years 1987, 1988 and 1989, and extracted the number of violations by each country in each of the three years in each of the seven categories listed below:-

1. Government inflicted deaths (excluding legal executions)
2. Disappearances of persons ascribed to government action
3. Legal executions
4. Torture of prisoners
5. Political prisoners and prisoners of conscience
6. Prisoners detained without trial
7. Prisoners held without a fair trial

In doing so, in order to avoid biasing our analysis, we have deliberately refrained from exercising any subjective judgement on our part on what

[1] Derbyshire and Derbyshire, eds., *Political Systems of the World*, (Chambers, London 1989).

constitutes a violation of human rights, but accepted without question the criteria accepted by Amnesty International. Nor have we attempted to assign relation weights to the different categories of violations. Furthermore, in the further interest of objectivity, we made sure that none of our scorers on human rights had taken part either in designing the scoring system on democracy or in the democracy scoring itself. In the interests of uniformity, we asked each human rights scorer to score all countries for one year.

The information in Amnesty International's report, due no doubt to the extreme difficulty in gathering data, is often not accurate enough to give other than just orders of magnitude for the numbers of violations. Thus, for example, some entries read 'many hundreds were killed' or 'there are thousands of political prisoners'. Further we have to recognize the fact that in a country like China with a population of over a billion, a thousand deaths do not have the same significance as the same number of deaths in a country with a population of a few thousand. We have therefore devised the following scoring systems. In each category 1 to 7 listed above, we take the number of violations detected and divide it by the total population of that country. If the number of violations is a few in ten million, we record two penalty points, and if a few in a million, we record three penalty points, and so on. For those of our readers who are familiar with mathematical jargon, this means that we are using a logarithmic scale to record the number of violations. The more penalty points a country accumulates, the worse is its human rights record.

First, for an overview of the general situation, we take each country and count the total number of penalty points, say P, incurred in the year in all seven categories 1 to 7. We then define a human rights rating of our own, the Forum rating F, as: $F = 10 - P$. The higher the value of F, the better the human rights record. The average F ratings over three years for the eight democracy grades are shown in Fig. 3. Again, as in Fig. 2, there is a clear indication that countries with a high democracy score have a better human rights rating.

To examine the records in more detail, let us divide the countries into a 'high-D group', those with a democracy score greater than 5, and a 'low-D group', containing all the rest. One sees then that the high-D group has human rights records far superior than those in the low-D group in each of the three years studied, as seen in the average F rating of the two groups shown in Table I, as well as in each of the seven categories, 1 to 7, of human rights violations, as seen in Table II, listing the average penalty points incurred. We stress that this large difference between the two groups of countries is obtained even without taking account of the probable large numbers of violations committed by undemocratic governments which remain undetected due to censorship and willful suppression of information.

Finally, to see what percentage of countries in each democracy grade may be considered as having a good human rights record, let us define for this purpose a 'good' record as a total of fewer than 7 penalty points in all seven categories of violation in all three years. (This represents on average fewer than one violation in each category per ten million of population in all three years). The percentage of countries in each democracy grade having a thus-defined 'good' human rights record is shown in Fig. 4. Again, one sees the high-D group of countries emerging as clear winners, with more than 80% passing as 'good'. One notes also that due to our scoring system based only on detected violations, the fact that in Fig. 4 some countries with low democracy rating are seen to have 'good' human rights records may just mean that they have not had their violations detected.

We recognize that our scoring system for democracy and human rights are both at present rather simplistic and our correlation analysis rather crude. However, the strong positive correlations seem quite unmistakeable. We therefore conclude with confidence that democratic countries have on average a better human rights record than undemocratic countries.

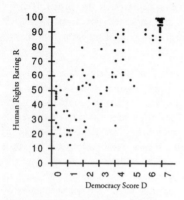

Figure 1. 'Scatter plot' of Human Rights Rating R from ref. 1 against our democracy score D. For each country one enters a point with R as ordinate and D as abscissa. One sees from this plot that more democratic countries with high D tend to have higher values of R, i.e. better human rights records.

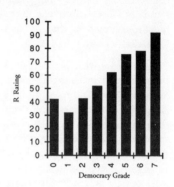

Figure 3. The average Forum Rating F for human rights is shown for countries in different democracy grades. One sees that more democratic countries in the higher D grades have on the average a higher F, i.e. fewer human rights violations in 1987–89, according to Amnesty International reports.

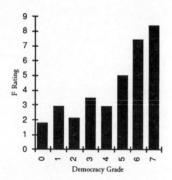

Figure 2. The average Human Rights Rating R is shown for countries in different democracy grades. Again, one sees that more democratic countries in the higher D grades have, on average, a higher R, i.e. better human rights records according to ref. 1.

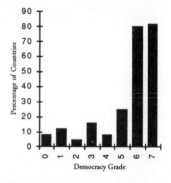

Figure 4. Shows the percentage of countries in each democracy grade deemed by the present analysis as having a 'good' human rights record in the three years 1987–89. More than 80% of the countries in grades 6 and 7 passed the test, far superior to the record for the lower grades.

Forum Rating	Low D	High D
1989	2.09	7.87
1988	2.39	8.23
1987	3.86	8.61

Table I. Compares the average Forum Human Rights Rating F for the 'high D' group of countries with democracy score D greater than S with that for the 'low D' group of countries with democracy score D less than or equal to S for each of the three years studied. The rating for the 'high D' group is far superior to that for the 'low D' group in all three years.

Penalty Points	Low D	High D
Deaths	1.11	0.25
Disappearances	0.37	0.04
Executions	0.63	0.29
Torture	0.68	0.15
Prisoners	2.64	0.80
Without Trial	1.16	0.19
Unfair Trial	0.61	0.04

Table II. Compares the average penalty points incurred by the 'low D' group of countries to that by the 'high D' group for human rights violations in each of the seven categories studied. It shows far fewer violations for the 'high D' group of countries which are deemed to have more democratic governments. Notice that the penalty points are recorded on a 'logarithmic scale' so that one penalty point higher means ten times more violations. Thus for example the fact that the 'low D' group has incurred almost one point more than the 'high D' group under 'Deaths' and almost two points more under 'Prisoners' means that on the average an undemocratic 'low D' government inflicts ten times more deaths on their people and holds a hundred times more political prisoners or prisoners of conscience than a democratic 'high D' government.

CENSORSHIP
AND
PROPAGANDA

MEDIA CENSORSHIP IN THE PEOPLE'S REPUBLIC OF CHINA[1]

MICHAEL SCHOENHALS

IT WOULD BE AN UNDERSTATEMENT to say that, as a political institution and fact of life in the People's Republic of China (PRC), censorship has not received the attention it deserves from outside observers, students and scholars. Not only have no books been written about it; the number of substantial articles dealing with how it does what it does have also been few and far in between.

In this short paper, I shall be looking at censorship in the PRC from three different angles. First, briefly, at some of the formal laws and statutes related to censorship that have been enacted by the PRC government and Chinese Communist Party (CCP) since 1949. Secondly, at the censorship praxis of the 1950s and Cultural Revolution decade (1966–76) which, for simplicity's sake, will be limited to an examination of censorship involving public discourse on people — political friends and foes, dead and living capitalists, rich peasants, revolutionaries, etc. — avoiding the grey area of censorship related to legitimate state secrets. Finally, I shall speculate about the present and future of censorship in China.

LAWS AND STATUTES

Most of the formal laws and statutes that govern the freedom of expression in the PRC do not at first sight appear excessively draconian, but resemble similar laws elsewhere. For example, the statutes concerning the censorship of printed matter released by the Standing Committee of the National People's Congress in November 1955, list six criteria that no book, magazine, etc. must violate if it is to appear legally. The first criterion is that printed matter must not 'oppose the people's democratic state, or violate current government policies, laws or statutes.' Secondly, it must not whip up ethnic or racist hatred; thirdly, it must not be against world peace or propagate imperialist aggression; fourthly, it must not reveal state secrets; fifthly, it must not advocate crime, be pornographic, harm public order,

[1] The research and writing of this paper were supported by a research grant from the Swedish Research Council for the Humanities and Social Sciences (HSFR).

etc; and finally, it must not violate the constitution.[1] If one looks only at the general wording of some of these criteria, they are vaguely similar to laws on pornography, state secrets etc. which were in operation in quite a few Western states at the time.

In the 1950s, the document just mentioned and a few others like it did not yet contain the reference to the 'leadership of the CCP' which later became obligatory. In the 1990s, the statutes that govern the freedom of expression in China have grown to nine in number. They are repeated in identical form in a number of legal texts, including a set of 'Temporary Regulations Governing Newspapers', from which they are translated below. Public discourse in the PRC media today must not:

(1) Instigate resistance or damage to the implementation of the constitution or the law

(2) Instigate the overthrow of the people's democratic dictatorship or damage to the socialist system, the division of the country, or armed rebellion or riots

(3) Instigate opposition to the leadership of the CCP

(4) Reveal state secrets, harm the safety or interests of the state

(5) Instigate ethnic or racist prejudice or hatred, or harm ethnic unity

(6) Damage social peace or instigate turmoil

(7) Propagate homicide, obscenity, pornography, feudal superstition or bogus science, abet crime or harm the physical and spiritual health of the young

(8) Slander or insult people

(9) Publish anything else not permitted by law[2]

The crucial point here, as every student of contemporary China knows, is the third regulation concerning the leadership of the CCP. In its application to political discourse it has become in effect a super-law: not only is it concerned with criticism of the CCP as the political party whose members hold the offices of government, but also with criticism of what the members of the 'leading' CCP say and do.

---

[1] *Zhonghua Renmin Gongheguo Xianxing Xinwen Chuban Fagui Huibian 1949–1990* [Collected current press and publishing laws and regulations of the People's Republic of China 1949–1990] (Renmin chubanshe, Beijing 1991), p. 3.
[2] ibid., p. 122.

To oppose anything publicly that is said or done by the leading members of the CCP is by the common interpretation and application of this super-law technically 'illegal'. The clause concerning the 'leadership of the CCP' automatically extends a quasi-legal status not only to any and all policies of the CCP Politburo, but also to remarks by individual CCP leaders. This phenomenon was already given symbolic recognition during the Cultural Revolution, when China's Supreme People's Court was rendered inoperative at the same time as the words of CCP Chairman Mao Zedong were referred to in the media as 'supreme instructions'.

In the early years of the PRC, the Central People's Government justified media censorship by pointing to the fact that the country was at war in Korea, and the CCP, technically speaking, still at war with the 'reactionary Guomindang regime' on Taiwan. Perhaps it is permissible to keep the press on a somewhat tighter reign than usual in such difficult times. But the CCP from the very beginning was far more indiscriminate in its censorship than was justified by the war. And, more importantly, when international tensions relaxed and the war ended, there was very little change on the domestic front, except for a brief flurry of 'liberalism' in the spring of 1957.

In the following examples of PRC censorship the common theme is people. What is being censored here are not cases of libel or blasphemy but, judged by any standard other than that applied by the CCP, trivialities. Still, at the time, these were regarded as genuine instances of opposition to, or distortion of Party policies and therefore by extension the Party's leading role.

FICTION AND FACT: CENSORSHIP IN THE 1950S

From the very beginning, any and all forms of public discourse in the PRC had to 'accord with the relevant policies of the party.' No writer, not even a poet or a novelist, had the right to use the idea that fiction was different from fact to defend him- or herself from political censorship in this respect. If a short story or novel was about events in the Chinese countryside in the not too distant past, it had to depict those events in a way that ultimately proved and propagated the correctness of the Party's rural policies. The same general rule applied to short stories about workers, poems about soldiers, and essays about hardworking intellectuals.

Writers who aspired to have their works published soon became only too well aware of what the Party censors demanded of them. But even in cases where they had done virtually everything possibly to ensure that their works contained no political errors, the censors would still catch them on technicalities. Take the case of Ding Ling, the highly acclaimed author and friend of Mao Zedong's from the days when the CCP leadership was still living in caves in the Yan'an hills. In the 1940s, she wrote a novel about land reform entitled *Taiyang zhao zai Sanggan He shang* [Sun Over the Sanggan River]. Its powerful depiction of landlords, peasants and communist cadres engaged in a struggle over land and livelihood eventually won her the Stalin Prize in 1951 and her novel was considered one of the best literary works of New China by communist and non-communist literary critics alike. Still, there were passages in it — its pre-1949 edition in particular — that prompted the censors to intervene.

In a work published in 1984 by a literary historian giving a minutely detailed account of the revision of consecutive editions of *Sun Over the Sanggan River*, the issue of the rich peasant–status of the fictional character Gu Yong is raised. In her original text, Ding Ling had written that Gu Yong 'employed very many casual laborers' and that he was consequently given a rich peasant status by the CCP. (Ding was, as she should have been, following the criteria for who was and who was not a rich peasant drawn up by the Jiangxi Soviet Central Government in 1933.) But, in the plot, Gu eventually becomes a 'positive character', undeserving of his rich peasant status. The problem, for the censor, if not necessarily for the reader, lay in the fact that *if* Gu indeed had employed 'very many' casual laborers, he *was* indeed a rich peasant according to the rules that applied in the 'real' world. Now, to have a rich peasant become a 'positive character', even in a work of fiction, was rather inappropriate. In the Party's understanding of class struggle, 'rich peasants' belonged to 'the enemy', together with 'landlords, reactionaries and "bad elements"'. The way out of this impasse was by way of revising the text to make it seem as if Gu's initial rich peasant status had been given him by mistake. When the Beijing shudian published *Sun Over the Sanggan River* in 1951, its editors made the necessary changes. They first added words to the effect that Gu Yong had only 'temporarily' employed people. Then they changed the number of people he had employed from 'very many' to 'some'. In this way it became quite obvious that Gu had not been a rich peasant in the first place, and his subsequent positive role no longer clashed with the Party's understanding or human nature. The literary historian, writing in 1984, makes the following observation in support of the revision: 'Literary works are by no means pamphlets for explaining policy, but they do fulfill a propaganda and educational function, and have to be historically accurate. For this reason, accounts in literary works must not contradict the relevant policies of the Party.'[1]

Journalists and others who wrote exclusively about people and events in the 'real' world were of course far more affected by the rule that nothing could 'contradict the relevant policies of the Party.' In Ding Ling's case, writing about land reform in the 1940s, the problem had been how to depict a fictitious peasant. For Chinese journalists writing about the nationalization of private enterprises in the mid–1950s, the problem was how to describe real 'flesh–and–blood' capitalists. In retrospect, it would appear as if the risk of committing 'errors' in these contexts must have been considerable.

In February 1956, the CCP Central Propaganda Department issued a general circular to all of China's media criticizing what it called the 'errors' of some newspapers in reporting the 'reform of bourgeois elements'. The Propaganda Department stressed that there were primarily two kinds of phenomena that were in need of instant rectification. The first, it said, was the frequent 'unprincipled flattery of capitalists'. For example, a journalist with the newspaper *Dagongbao* [L'Impartial] had recently described one minor capitalist, saying 'from his chubby looks you can tell right away that here is someone who is enthusiastic about working for the public good.' Another capitalist had been described by the same journalist as 'the wearer of a pair of golden–rimmed spectacles, a refined and courteous person.' According to the Propaganda Department, this kind of 'boasting on behalf of capitalists is obviously wrong, and violates the Party's policy vis-a-vis the bourgeoisie, of educating them and transforming them.' The second phenomenon in need of immediate rectification was the exact opposite of the first. It concerned the Party's policy of trying to win over some 'big' capitalists for the socialist cause — people like Rong Yiren, formerly the owner of the Sangsong Cotton Mills and Fuxin Flour Company in Shanghai, and since 1953 vice-chairman of the National Federation of Industry and Commerce. To 'expose indiscriminately' the uglier sides of the past of these so-called 'core elements of the bourgeoisie' was 'inappropriate'. The Propaganda Department told the media that 'it is not necessary to pay special attention to their "shady deals", or to make them engage in public self-criticism because of their ugly history of exploitation and degenerate debauchery.' As in the case of the small or ordinary capitalists who were to be exposed, rather than flattered, this differential treatment accorded the big capitalists was rooted in the policy needs of the

[1] Gong Mingde, Taiyang Zhao Zai Sanggan He Shang *Xiugai Jianping* [Notes and comments on the revision of *Sun Shines Over the Sanggan River*] (Hunan renmin chubanshe, Changsha 1984), pp. 16–7.

CCP. The party itself would look bad if journalists were to be allowed to use the word 'degenerate' to refer to the very same people for whom Mao Zedong and Zhou Enlai reserved the label 'great patriotic industrialist'.[1]

In 1957, thousands of journalists and writers of fiction — including Ding Ling — who had had trouble with censorship since 1949 were labelled 'rightists' by the CCP leadership, dismissed from their posts, and sent to labour camps. A sizable number were released and even given their jobs back in the early 1960s, but with the advent of the Cultural Revolution the situation rapidly went from bad to worse.

FROM COMRADES TO NON–PERSONS: CENSORSHIP IN THE CULTURAL REVOLUTION

The Cultural Revolution witnessed the indiscriminate persecution of an unprecedented number of outspoken citizens who sometimes had done no more than raise doubts about the wisdom of the policies of the Party in private conversation. It also resulted in purges of a steady stream of high-level CCP leaders, beginning with the PLA chief of staff in the winter of 1965–66 and ending with the arrest of the 'Gang of Four' in the autumn of 1976. In each case, one of the first things that happened as part of the purges was the transformation, by way of central decree, of the person purged from a 'comrade' to a non–person. A disgraced person no longer had the right to make his voice heard. Pictures were removed from walls, books were removed from bookshelves, heads blackened out in photographs, samples of calligraphy were sand-blasted off the bases of statues, and so on. It did not matter if the person purged had been 'ultra-left' or 'ultra-right', he or she could now only be referred to with the help of some derogatory label.

This particular aspect of the Cultural Revolution was highly visible, and as such commented upon in the foreign media at the time. Details about the decrees that initiated it, in each instance, have however only become known in recent years. Through these bureaucratic communications we observe censorship politics assuming a wave-like form, as one group of leaders after the other is toppled.

---

[1] Zhongguo Shehui Kexueyuan Xinwen Yanjiusuo, ed., *Zhongguo Gongchandang Xinwen Gongzuo Wenjian Huibian* [Collected CCP documents on the work of the press], 3 vols. (Xinhua chubanshe, Beijing 1980), vol. 2, pp. 496–7.

A directive dealing specifically with works by or in some other way linked to the first casualties of the Cultural Revolution was issued by the Ministry of Culture in July 1966. The senior party leaders who signed it were Liu Shaoqi — acting as the head of the CCP while Mao Zedong was absent from the capital — and Tao Zhu, director of the CCP Central Propaganda Department. It banned the further publication and distribution of works by such 'anti-Party and anti-socialist elements' as Beijing's mayor, Peng Zhen, the former minister of culture and director of the Central Propaganda Department Lu Dingyi, and the chairman of the Chinese Writers' Association Zhou Yang. It also banned the further publication and distribution of 'any and all poisonous weeds that have been criticized by name in the press, including literary and academic works.'[1]

Interestingly enough, this first directive still permitted bookshops to sell any remaining stock they might have of the above categories of books. When Liu Shaoqi and Tao Zhu were themselves purged in the winter of 1966–67, this fact promptly became one of their many 'heinous crimes'. It was claimed that they had approved the continued sale of 'poisonous weeds' in spite of the fact that 'the revolutionary masses everywhere had demanded that bookshops stop selling them immediately.'[2]

Liu Shaoqi and Tao Zhu were the two most senior of the Cultural Revolution's second wave of casualties. In a way similar to how they themselves had ordered the removal of their enemies' words from the shelves of China's bookshops, their own faces were now ordered removed from the images to be shown in China's movie theatres and on television. During a visit to the Central Newsreel Studios in February 1967, Defence Minister Lin Biao's 'specially appointed consultant to the PLA in cultural affairs' — Mao Zedong's wife Jiang Qing — told the studio staff:

> The first time I saw the film about [the CCP leadership's review of the Red Guard during] the National Day celebrations [on 1 October 1966], I thought it was outrageous, and had it sent back. The second time was even worse and we had it sent back once again. What kind of stuff is this?... The film about the Chairman reviewing the Red Guard flies in the face of the spirit of the Central Committee's 11th Plenum. It prettifies Liu [Shaoqi], Deng [Xiaoping] and Tao [Zhu]....

---

[1] *Liu Shaoqi Fangeming Xiuzhengzhuyi Yanlun Huibian* [Collection of counter-revolutionary revisionist statements by Liu Shaoqi], (Zhongguo kexueyuan geming lishi yanjiusuo, Beijing 1967), p. 99.
[2] ibid.

Do you think you could cut out the frames that have Liu, Deng and Tao in them from the film about Chairman Mao reviewing the Red Guard for the first, second and third time?... You must make Zhao Xinchu [who is in charge of films at the Ministry of Culture] confess how he prettified Liu, Deng and Tao. You should struggle with him properly, and you should then strike down every one of those types you struggle with.[1]

During the years that followed, it was not possible to mention Liu Shaoqi's name in print without adding that he had been a 'renegade, traitor and scab'. His picture did not appear in print or on television once between 1967 and 1979.

The Cultural Revolution's third wave of high-level casualties, purged in 1968, included a group of senior PLA officers, whose alleged crimes included using the printed word to 'slander maliciously and attack Vice-chairman Lin Biao.' In this case, the problem was no longer what they had written, but rather what they had *not* written or permitted to be written. One particular 'crime' committed by the political commissar of the PLA Air Force — the 'big careerist, big schemer, big renegade and big counter-revolutionary revisionist' Yu Lijin — had to do with the design of Mao badges. According to an investigation carried out at the time by members of the PLA Air Force:

In January 1968, the Air Force Research Department had designed a [Mao] badge for the Second Air Force Congress of Activists in the Study of Chairman Mao's Works. As part of the design, they had included Vice-chairman Lin's inscription for the navy ['Navigating the great ocean, we rely on the helmsman; making revolution, we rely on Mao Zedong Thought']. [Air Force Commander] Comrade Wu Faxian agreed, but Yu Lijin brazenly asked for the inscription to be removed.[2]

In the semiotic context of Mao badges, not only the text of any inscription, but also the direction in which Mao's face looked was of direct concern to vigilant radicals. A badge designer in Huhehot, Inner Mongolia, was persecuted for being responsible for the only known Mao badge that has Mao looking not towards the left, but towards the right. This was in-

[1] *Wuxian Fengguang Zai Xianfeng: Jiang Qing Tongzhi Guanyu Wenyi Geming de Jianghua* [On perilous peaks dwells beauty in her infinite variety: Talks on revolution in the arts by comrade Jiang Qing], (Nankai daxue weidong, Tianjin 1968), pp. 328–29.
[2] Dong Baocun, *Yang-Yu-Fu Shijian* [The Yang-Yu-Fu incident], (Jiefangjun chubanshe, Beijing 1988), p. 135.

terpreted as suggesting that Mao sympathized with the political 'right' rather than the 'left'.[1]

Lin Biao became a victim of the Cultural Revolution in 1971. After his fall, the kind of inscriptions that Yu had not wanted to see on the badges issued to the PLA Air Force became part of a corpus of texts referred to as 'Lin–poison' in official party and government documents. The removal of this 'poison' from the discourse did not just mean banning a few hundred slogans, or pulping a few tonnes of books, it was a far more ambitious undertaking.

> One department store in Liuan county mobilized the masses to the fullest... and cleared out altogether 290,000 items of 117 different kinds of merchandise with Lin Biao's calligraphy, words or picture on them. Some 184,900 items of 79 different kinds of merchandise were put on the market again after having been subjected to technical treatment... Some units, however, still openly sell porcelain mugs and other merchandise with Lin Biao's calligraphy on them,... and this has an extremely bad political impact among the masses.[2]

In the fall of 1976, the surviving radicals who, together with Mao, had launched the Cultural Revolution ten years earlier became the last victims of this 'great movement'. And once more, in precisely the same way as in 1966, 1967, 1968 and 1971, their faces were removed from the pages of the *Renmin Huabao* [China Pictorial], and their names removed from the list of 'comrades' and moved onto the list of 'enemies of the people'. In a Central Committee circular, it was decreed that:

> The distribution, sale and mailing of newspapers and magazines... containing photographs, drawings or cartoon strips of, works, articles or speeches by, or quotations from the revisionist utterances and propagations of the utterances of the 'Gang of Four' is to cease...

> The showing of films, documentaries and videos in which the 'Gang of Four' appear is to cease.[3]

---

[1] Sang Hua, 'Canyang Ruxue' [Remnants of the sun like blood], *Dushu*, no. 11, 1991, p. 69.
[2] 'Anhui Sheng Shangyeju Guanyu Chedi Qingcha Chuli You Lin Biao Yihuo Shouji, Wenzi, Tuhua de Shangpin de Tongzhi' [Circular of the Anhui provincial Bureau of Commerce concerning the thorough disposal of merchandise with the calligraphy, words or pictures of Lin Biao and his gang on them] (19 June 1973), p. 1.
[3] *Zhongfa* [76] 18, quoted in Michael Schoenhals, 'Weeding out the "Gang of Four"', *Index on Censorship*, no. 6 (1988), p. 12.

CENSORSHIP TODAY

In the 1980s, the Chinese media were able to publish things that in an earlier age would have been unthinkable. In literature and the arts, there was a freedom to experiment with new topics and new themes unprecedented since 1949. The reasons for this broadening of the scope of what could be expressed and communicated publicly were complex. In the case of the publishing industry, for instance, it would be a mistake to reduce them solely to economic factors, i.e. that in order to survive in a gradually more market-oriented economy, one simply had to become more daring, or not be able to attract readers.

But what did not happen at any point in the 1980s was the clear and unequivocal re-definition, by the CCP, of the existing parameters of freedom of expression. Rather, the political directives addressing this issue became gradually more ambiguous, and more open to differing interpretations. In one directive, circulated by the CCP Central Secretariat, the mass media's parameters were formulated as follows: 'It is impermissible to upset the overall situation of stability and unity, or shake the progressive confidence of the popular masses.'[1]

Ultimately, this view of what the media may or may not do is a reflection of Confucian and Leninist approaches to government, which both aim towards an ultimate goal of social order and harmony. The rights of the media's producers and consumers alike are granted from on high, and only to the extent that they serve the overall societal good. Few Chinese intellectuals raise fundamental objections to the setting of such parameters. Controversy tends to centre upon how words like 'upset' and 'shake' are to be defined and put into practice. In private, there are also the interesting questions of whether a situation of stability and unity really exists to be 'upset', and whether the public really has any confidence to be 'shaken', but in public this is a given.

In the spring of 1989, many intellectuals had come to the conclusion that the way by which China's media would help preserve domestic social order and harmony in the long run was by being more open. Hu Jiwei, former editor-in-chief of the *Renmin Ribao* [People's Daily], stated that freedom of the press would enhance social stability by allowing people to vent their frustrations, improving communication and trust among different sectors

[1] *Shiyi Jie San Zhong Quanhui Yilai Dang de Xuanchuan Gongzuo Wenxian Xuanbian* [Selected documents on the propaganda work of the Party since the third plenum of the eleventh Central Committee], (Zhonggong zhongyang dangxiao chubanshe, Beijing 1989), p. 384.

of society, increasing public confidence in the CCP and contributing to the cause of building socialist democracy.[1] And for a brief period in May 1989, there was indeed very little censorship to speak of in newspapers like the *Renmin Ribao*. China's foremost investigative journalist Liu Binyan has spoken of those days saying that 'press freedom in China existed', but 'for only three days.'[2]

Since June 1989, there has been a different situation. Public discourse on democracy, and talk of how the social stratum that liked to call itself 'the servants of the people' turned into 'the masters of the people', is no longer permitted. Those presently in control of China's media subscribe to the notion that it is by exercising maximum restraint that the press is able to contribute to the strengthening of 'popular confidence' in the bright future of socialism. They believe that nothing is less conducive to 'unity and stability' than a 'free' press. The 'masses', they argue, would only become 'confused' by it.

I shall let the father of CCP censorship Hu Qiaomu — the first director of the Government Press Administration, once Mao's political secretary, and long-time ideological advisor to Deng Xiaoping — spell out the ideological tenet that informs the Party's curtailment of the freedom of expression. In defense of the praxis of censoring discourse that centres on democracy and corrupt officialdom, he explained to a gathering of propaganda officials in 1983 that:

> Unless we really have solid evidence of a small number of people actually having pissed and shat on the heads of the people, we must not carelessly speak of the servants of the people having turned into the masters of the people. Because, otherwise, the distinction between socialism on the one hand and feudalism and capitalism on the other will have disappeared.[3]

Strict political and ideological controls over what is said in public are essential not only to the preservation of domestic 'unity and stability' and popular 'confidence', but to the very definition of what constitutes social-

[1] Judy Polumbaum, 'To Protect or Restrict? Points of Contention in China's Draft Press Law', a paper presented at the AAS Annual Meeting in Chicago, April 5–8, 1990, p. 29.
[2] Quoted in Frank Tan, 'The *People's Daily:* Politics and Popular Will — Journalistic Defiance in China During the Spring of 1989', *Pacific Affairs*, vol. 63 no. 2 (Summer 1990), p. 153.
[3] 'Hu Qiaomu Tongzhi Guanyu Xuexi *Deng Xiaoping Wenxuan* de Jianghua' [Comrade Hu Qiaomu's talk on studying the *Selected Works of Deng Xiaoping*], *Xueshu Yanjiu Dongtai*, vol. 150 (1983), p. 3.

ism, and the distinction between it and other stages in the history of mankind, such as feudalism and capitalism. If China's newspapers were able to say that the CCP leadership is pissing and shitting on the heads of the people, then this in itself would suggest to Hu Qiaomu et al. that socialism with Chinese characteristics is on the way to 'peacefully evolving' into its own negation. Therefore, it is not permitted.

As one Chinese journalist put it, the 'fundamental principle of socialism is that the people are masters of the country, yet the masters are not supposed to criticize their servants.'[1] This situation — wherein the CCP remains in power and committed to socialism thus defined — will in all likelihood persist for some time. Eventually, once the Party's elders pass from the scene, we shall no doubt witness fierce criticism of some of them. Some will almost certainly be publicly accused of indeed having defecated 'on the heads of the people'. But this criticism will not be freedom of expression, any more than was the carefully orchestrated denunciation of the 'Gang of Four' subsequent to Mao Zedong's death in 1976.

The trend towards a market-driven economy in parts of China has already had and will continue to have an impact on the form and contents of the entertainment sector and 'low-brow' mass media in particular. We already see a Chinese press at greater liberty to publish what in the past would have been condemned by believers in a purer form of socialism as petit-bourgeois trash. On television, soap operas like the mini-series *Bianjibu de Gushi* [Stories from the Editorial Board] now contain a fair amount of social and even political commentary. How long this trend will last is hard to predict, but over the next few years, we shall probably witness a partial convergence of the Chinese and Hong Kong-Taiwan media.

I do not believe we shall see, in the near future, the end of the censorship praxis that has curtailed the freedom of expression in China since 1949. Even in the unlikely event of the present émigré movement of 'liberal' champions of a free press returning to China to redefine some of its political institutions, we shall not see the emergence and survival of a Chinese equivalents of *The Independent*, or a Hyde Park Corner off Tiananmen Square. Former propaganda officials within that movement would quickly, I believe, find persistently dissenting voices unbearable, and move to have them silenced — this time, no doubt, in defence of 'a fledgling democracy', rather than 'socialism'. Genuine change will only come gradually in China, over a period of time stretching far into the twenty-first century.

---

[1] Quoted in Polumbaum, op cit., p. 23.

CENSORSHIP & SELF-CENSORSHIP IN CONTEMPORARY CHINESE LITERATURE

BONNIE S MCDOUGALL

IT HAS LONG BEEN COMMONPLACE to attribute the poor quality of contemporary Chinese writing to censorship, even though very little has been written about the actual operation of censorship in contemporary China (by which is meant here the Chinese mainland since 1949). As early as 1963, however, following a conference on Chinese communist literature at Ditchley, Cyril Birch pointed out that 'It is not at all to be taken for granted that control is disastrous for literature'.[1] It is possible to point to successful literary works that have been produced under censorship: in our own times, for instance, in the former Soviet Union and Eastern European countries.[2]

In the broader sense that Birch is evidently referring to, we might also wish to take into account systems of control in premodern times: Ming and Qing China, or Tsarist Russia. This is, however, to distract attention from one of the major differences between now and the past, that is, the significantly firmer and wider systems of control that are distinctive to the twentieth century and are instituted by what are generally known as totalitarian states. In post–1949 China, as in the former Soviet Union and the Eastern European bloc before the collapse of their communist parties, the state managed to penetrate and control society as a whole. This is not to deny the existence of inefficiencies in control mechanisms and temporary

1 Cyril Birch, 'The Particle of Art', *China Quarterly*, no. 13 (March 1963), pp. 3–14, quote p. 3.
2 For an exceptionally informative, stimulating and comprehensive survey of literary and other censorship in the former Soviet Union, see Martin Dewhirst and Robert Farrell eds., *The Soviet Censorship* (Scarecrow Press, Metuchen, N.J. 1973); for more recent information, see Marianna Tax Choldin and Maurice Friedberg eds., *The Red Pencil: Artists, Scholars, and Censors in the USSR* (Unwin Hyman, Boston 1989). For Poland, see Jane Leftwich Curry, *The Black Book of Polish Censorship* (Random House, New York 1984). For Czechoslovakia, see Václav Havel, 'The Power of the Powerless' (1978) and 'Six Asides about Culture' (1984) in Jan Vladislav, ed.,*Václav Havel, or Living in Truth* (Faber and Faber, London 1987), pp. 36–122 & 123–35. Miklós Haraszti's *The Velvet Prison: Artists under State Socialism* (Penguin, London 1989), on censorship in Hungary, is badly flawed; see below, page. 79, n.1.

aberrations caused by factional strife, or the fact that many of the state's citizens may appear to acquiesce in their condition — which is not a justification of control but another aspect of it. Observers have sometimes been led to overlook the operation of censorship and self-censorship because of these factors, ignoring the mostly invisible networks of control. This article concentrates on three aspects of censorship and self-censorship in a literary context in contemporary China: as cultural and ideological constructs; as structures and mechanisms; and as operational elements in literary values.

CULTURE AND IDEOLOGY IN CENSORSHIP AND SELF-CENSORSHIP

An examination of the nature of censorship and self-censorship in contemporary China might start with an attempt to determine whether it is a predominately Chinese or a predominately communist condition. One phenomenon that supports the contention that it is associated with communist ideology rather than with the cultural traditions of countries as distinct as Russia and China is the adoption of self-censorship by self-professed socialist critics in non-communist countries such as Britain and America, as shown in the following two examples.

In a book published in the early 1970s,[1] the Scottish critic David Craig concludes his chapter on socialism and literature with the following remarks: 'When I look at socialism and its literature for myself, I find that it includes Brecht and MacDiarmid [...] Lu Hsun in China, Silone in Italy, Neruda in Chile, the range of Soviet masters of fiction long and short [...] most of the new dramatists in Britain and [Adrian] Mitchell in our poetry — to say nothing of the new cultures of Hungary, Poland, Czechoslovakia, China and the rest, which will indeed have suffered seriously under the "ice-age" but which must stand high on the agenda of anyone concerned with literature until he has honestly tried them for himself.'[2]

This curiously evasive statement — it is not clear whether Craig has read the literatures of the 'new cultures' himself or not — draws no distinction between socialist writing in countries where socialist rule is or is not established. Throughout this book, for all its admirable internationalism, we are not given any example of a writer publishing between 1949 and 1969 in

[1] David Craig, *The Real Foundations: Literature and Social Change* (Chatto & Windus, London 1973); see especially the chapter entitled 'The New Poetry of Socialism', pp. 213–29.
[2] ibid., p. 229.

China whom Craig would stand against Lu Xun (who is mentioned several times), nor of the 'new kinds of [Soviet] writers who have come to the fore'.[1] Earlier in the same chapter, however, Craig notes that 'even in the best work [of a Soviet writer] there will be veins of unreality, stiffnesses, palpable surrogates for things that were crying out to be rendered [...] That last example [of the undue part played by coincidence in novels by Pasternak and Dudintsev] is especially significant for it takes us to the heart of the disability — like some pervasive nervous disease — which crept through Soviet writers precisely as they tried to organise experience into a large continuum such as Western writers no longer had the spirit to attempt'.[2] This reference to censorship and self-censorship in the former Soviet Union combines an instance of self-censorship about Soviet writers with palpable disinformation about Western writers.

A similiar wilfulness exists on the other side of the Atlantic, exemplified in Fredric Jameson's references to 'socialist culture' in China. In an essay comparing Wang Meng and Wang Wenxing, for instance, Jameson describes the 'reinvention of lived memory' in Wang Meng's post-Cultural Revolution fiction as an articulation of 'shared experience' in a 'collective and historical way' and looks forward to a time 'when a socialist culture has evolved to the point where it has its own long historical tradition and where its formal originality has become visible and distinct...',[3] glossing over the 'shared experience' of censorship and self-censorship which caused Wang Meng to shape his fiction in a 'collective and historical way'.

A general critique of the cultural caricatures produced by Jameson in his use of the Maoist category 'the Third World' has already appeared and does not need repeating here.[4] Jameson makes specific references to China in another essay, 'The Cultural Logic of Late Capitalism' (1984).[5] The first is elicited by 'China', a poem by an American writer, about which Jameson writes: 'Many things could be said about this interesting exercise in discontinuities; not the least paradoxical is the re-emergence here across these disjointed sentences of some more unified global meaning. Indeed,

[1] ibid., p. 226.
[2] ibid., p. 227.
[3] Fredric Jameson, 'Literary Innovation and Modes of Production: A Commentary', *Modern Chinese Literature*, vol. 1 no. 1 (September 1984), pp. 67–77; quotes pp. 76–77.
[4] See Aijaz Ahmad, 'Jameson's Rhetoric of Otherness and the "National Allegory"', *Social Text*, no. 17 (Fall 1987), pp. 3–25, on Jameson's 'Third-World Literature in the Era of Multinational Capitalism', *Social Text*, no. 15 (Fall 1986), pp. 64–88.
[5] Reprinted as chapter one in *Postmodernism, or, the Cultural Logic of Late Capitalism* (Verso, London 1991).

insofar as this is in some curious and secret way a political poem, it does seem to capture something of the excitement of the immense, unfinished social experiment of the New China — unparalleled in world history — the unexpected emergence, between the two superpowers, of "number three", the freshness of a whole new object world produced by human beings in some new control over their collective destiny; the signal event, above all, of a collectivity which has become a new "subject of history" and which, after the long subjection of feudalism and imperialism, again speaks in its own voice, for itself, as though for the first time.'[1] The second reference is to Barthes' pun on the word 'Sinité', 'as some Disney-EPCOT "concept" of China'.[2]

Given Jameson's penchant for approaching Chinese history and culture through a Western cultural artefact, it is not surprising that his comments on China are either misinformed or simply nonsense.[3] For the purpose of this paper, the significant word in the passage quoted above is 'unfinished', which seems to stand as a kind of censored apology for the devastation to Chinese literature (not to mention Chinese lives) which resulted from this 'social experiment'. Even when Jameson first used the expression 'the incomplete Chinese experiment with a "proletarian" cultural revolution' in 1981,[4] the facts about the Cultural Revolution were already widely known; this kind of evasion in 1984 is even more inexcusable.

Since there is no state censorship of Marxist, Maoist or other socialist literary criticism in the United States or United Kingdom, Craig's and Jameson's oblique references to state censorship and self-censorship in the former Soviet Union and in China may be regarded as a form of self-censorship — in sympathy perhaps to the self-censoring writers in those countries. When we compare the Chinese to the former Soviet or Eastern European experience, however, very distinct differences become evident. Although state censorship was strictly enforced in the former socialist bloc for periods of up to seventy years, there grew up alongside it a substantial body of dissident, unoffical and underground literature. The question is

[1] ibid., p. 29.
[2] ibid., p. 19.
[3] For even more egregious misunderstandings, see his essay 'Periodizing the 60s' in *The Ideologies of Theory, Essays 1971–1986*, vol. 2, *Syntax of History* (Routledge, London 1988), pp. 178–208, esp. pp. 174, 188–89. Like Craig, Jameson cites Lu Xun, once only and then in a misleading context (see Jameson, *Signatures of the Visible* (Routledge, New York 1990), p. 4), but there is no evidence of knowledge of other Chinese writers except as in the 1984 commissioned article for *Modern Chinese Literature* cited above.
[4] Fredric Jameson, *The Political Unconscious: Narrative as a Socially Symbolic Act* (Methuen, London 1981), p. 95.

why in the twenty-five years between the establishment of Communist Party rule in China and the last phase of the Cultural Revolution, very little writing of any merit appeared either inside or outside the system.[1]

Since the end of the Cultural Revolution, Chinese intellectuals have been much occupied by this problem. The former Hong Kong writer Sun Longji in 1982 was one of the first to associate contemporary dependent behaviour with the Confucian tradition, suggesting that the Chinese as a whole are for cultural reasons 'particularly receptive to authoritarianism',[2] while the Taiwan dissident Bo Yang repeated much the same diagnosis two years later.[3] Liu Binyan, in a lecture given in the US in early 1989, commented that 'China's intellectuals were far more compliant in their dealings with the Communist Party than those of the Soviet Union and Eastern Europe', adding that in China, 'The appeal of name, position and material benefits is so strong among some intellectuals that it can overcome the desire for truth and lead to a willing sacrifice of individual talent'.[4] Liu associates this phenomenon with traditional Chinese culture — although he does not refer to Confucianism by name — and notes the high status and moral leadership enjoyed by scholars in traditional Chinese society.[5]

An unconventional approach to this debate comes from Liang Congjie, who goes beyond the standard gestures to 'the Confucian tradition' and looks towards popular, unofficial culture for the phenomenon of submission to authority. In a paper called 'The Tired Self of the Chinese Intellectuals', Liang notes firstly that the gradually intensifying demand for the 'elimination of the self' (*wu si*) in the first thirty years of Communist rule differs only in degree from the Confucian imperative to 'restrain

---

[1] For an account of the origins and nature of dissident literature in China, see McDougall, 'Dissent Literature: Official and Nonofficial Literature In and about China in the Seventies', *Contemporary China*, vol. 3 no. 4 (Winter 1979), pp. 49–79.

[2] See excerpts from Sun Longji's *Zhongguo wenhua de 'shenceng jiegou'* [The 'deep structure' of Chinese culture], translated in Geremie Barmé and John Minford, eds., *Seeds of Fire: Chinese Voices of Conscience* (Far Eastern Economic Review, Hong Kong 1986); quote from p. 311.

[3] See excerpt from Bo Yang's 'Choulou de Zhongguoren' [The ugly Chinaman], in *Seeds of Fire*, ibid., pp. 168–76.

[4] Liu Binyan, *China's Crisis, China's Hope: Essays from an Intellectual in Exile*, translated by Howard Goldblatt (Harvard University Press, Cambridge, Mass. 1990), pp. 41–43. See also his paper in this collection.

[5] I have attempted to explore this legacy in 'Self Cultivation as Group Justification: Narrative Voice in Wang Anyi's "Romances"', paper for the conference on 'The Self and Social Order', East–West Center, August 1991; to be published in the conference proceedings.

oneself in order to reestablish social righteousness' (*ke ji fu li*).[1] Liang Congjie does not fall into the trap of justifying Communist Party denigration of the self on the grounds of historical continuity, however. Instead, he points out that alongside the straightlaced, moralistic Confucian texts there also existed handbooks of popular philosophy such as *Xi shi xian wen* [Valuable sayings of the past; fl. 18th–19th century], which advised 'restraining the self' not for the sake of society or abstract virtue but for one's own protection in a world where being upright was not always rewarded as the upright would have wished it were. Among the sage advice offered by this useful manual are the following injunctions:

'Just sweep away the snow in front of your gate; don't bother about the frog on your neighbour's roof.'

'Tell people only one third of what could be said.'

'Never reveal all that's in your mind.'

'The bird which stretches out its head will be shot first.'

'Learn how to behave from the turtle; withdraw your head into your shell whenever possible.'

This kind of popular wisdom, whose late 20th century spokeman might be Garrison Keillor, is by no means exclusive to China and Chinese intellectuals. But if times were hard on the incautious scholar in Qing China, his 20th century descendant was in an even more precarious situation. Whatever the contribution of culture and ideology towards the phenomenon of censorship, part of the reason for self-censorship must be a basic instinct for survival. In this context, it should be useful to consider the nature of the censorship system itself.

THE STRUCTURE AND MECHANICS OF CENSORSHIP AND SELF-CENSORSHIP

One reason why censorship in China has been neglected by observers is that it operates most effectively as a pre-publication mechanism, in distinction to the much cruder post-publication banning of books that regularly gives rise to highly publicised scandals in Britain (for instance, *Lady Chatterley's Lover*, the schoolkids issue of *Oz* and *Spycatcher*). Pre-publication censorship is by its nature unobtrusive, and documentary proof of its

---

[1]Liang Congjie, 'The Tired Self of the Chinese Intellectuals', paper for the conference on 'The Self and Social Order', East–West Center, August 1991; to be published in the conference proceedings.

existence was up until very recently virtually impossible to obtain: most evidence is anecdotal, from interested parties, or inferential.

Some anecdotes about the operation of literary censorship I can supply from my own experience working as a translator and editor for the Foreign Languages Press in Beijing in the early 1980s. In 1981, for instance, I was assigned Wang Meng's 'Chun zhi ge' [Voices of Spring] for translation into English for the magazine *Chinese Literature*,[1] but the version passed on to me from the central editorial office contained several deletions and substitutions — for the sake of the foreign reader, it was explained. One substitution was the generic 'opera arias' for 'Yang Zirong's arias' (Yang Zirong being a character in the model revolutionary opera *Zhiqu Weihushan* [Taking Tiger Mountain by Strategy]). It seemed to me that even a reader without the faintest idea who Yang Zirong was (unlikely, given the nature of *Chinese Literature* readers in 1982) would not have any difficulty in working out from the context that the reference was to arias from Beijing Opera (revolutionary or otherwise); and I was concerned that the substitution removed both colour and meaning from the text. Since the Chinese editors failed to grasp the very elementary point that readers do not need to understand the exact meaning of every word in fiction (whether in translation or not), it seemed quite obviously a case of crass interference. (It was also possible, but not very likely, that the editors were anxious about sending out wrong signals by permitting a reference to a Cultural Revolution product.)

Further into the same text there was a straight deletion: 'the long queues of people in front of the men's and women's lavatories waiting to have a pee' was reduced to 'the long queues of people'. The deletion could have been made from prudery about basic body functions, except for the frequency of urinating children in Chinese feature films released for export in the 1980s; instead, I believe it was a case of the editors being anxious lest foreign readers regard China as backward because of the inadequacy of lavatory facilities at a major provincial railway station on the eve of Chinese New Year.

Eventually all the deletions and substitutions were removed and the original text restored. It was only much later that it occurred to me that I could be accused of having 'censored' the operation of censorship (the triviality of the examples not being at issue) at the Foreign Languages Press. Although in this case I don't believe this to have been the case, in another example (still trivial, but non-literary) I took on the role of censor myself: that is, I

[1] Published in *Chinese Literature*, Spring 1982, pp. 23–36.

successfully urged the deletion of a passage from a guide to tourist attractions in Beijing on the preparation of fish to be eaten live at the Tingliguan restaurant in the Summer Palace, on the grounds that English-speaking tourists were more likely to be repelled than attracted by the prospect.

These examples are more to do with taste or understanding rather than straight political issues, but it is easy to see how this kind of interference can reduce a literary text to something pallid and bland, an apt description of most of the texts produced since 1949. (A Western analogy might be situation comedies on commerical television.) In some ways, this can be even more frustrating to the author than deletions or proscriptions of politically sensitive materials, to the point where the more imaginative and adventurous writers begin to find silence a more bearable alternative.

A detailed account of editorial-level censorship has been made by Richard King in regard to the author Zhu Lin, whose career he has followed closely since their first meeting in 1979.[1] In an article called 'System and Text in Contemporary China', [2] King refers to several examples of pre- and post-publication censorship during the 1980s. Noting for instance the continued availability on the black market of the Chinese translation of *Lady Chatterley's Lover* after it was banned immediately upon publication in the spring of 1987, he also draws attention to the supposition that the ban was placed for diplomatic reasons rather than prudery or sexual hygiene; the local authorities read the title as *Mrs Thatcher's Lover* and were fearful of repercussions to Sino-British relations.

For Zhu Lin's story 'Guole Qingming hua bu hao' [The Festival of Graves],[3] King compares the printed version in *Shanghai Literature* with a manuscript version given to him by the author. The condition and status of the manuscript version are not closely defined, but it is implied that it is

---

[1] See 'In the Translator's Eye: Richard King on the Significance of Zhu Lin', *Modern Chinese Literature*, Winter 1988, pp. 171–76.

[2] Published as 'Systeme et texte en Chine contemporaine', *Cahiers du Centre d'Etudes de l'Asie de l'Est*, no. 7, 1989; I am referring to the unpublished English version in cyclostyled format. A rather different account of the censorship in *Lady Chatterley's Lover* is given in Yi Chen, 'Publishing in China in the Post-Mao Era: The Case of *Lady Chatterley's Lover*', *Asian Survey*, vol. 32 no. 6 (June 1992), pp. 568–82, which appeared while this article was in press.

[3] *Shanghai wenxue*, no. 12, 1987, pp. 47–52.

identical with that submitted to the magazine.[1] The main force of the deletions noted by King (who gives several examples but not the complete list) is to soften the portrayal of an old Party cadre whose arrogant behaviour in the past has brought about her disgrace in the present; some of the protagonist's jaundiced reflections on current economic policies are also deleted. In King's account, these deletions weaken a powerful description of a wholly recognizable and significant social phenomenon, simply for the sake of showing the Communist Party in a better light. King also gives an example of a cut made for purely literary reasons, the sort that any responsible editor would want to make.[2]

I have no doubt whatsoever that King is correct in his assumption that the first set of cuts he describes were made at editorial level to avoid the disapproval of the authorities — as much as one can ever be sure in speculating on intentions. I am less convinced that the excisions damage the story, whatever the motives of the censors. Zhu Lin's encounter with the apparatus of censorship must have been distressing, and King presents her case persuasively, but given that she is an interested party, a more detailed and objective account might have been more helpful.

An example of inferential evidence of censorship is the publication of Bei Dao's poems in the Chinese literary press during the years 1979 to 1984. Bei Dao first gained a devoted public during the Cultural Revolution when his dissident poems were circulated underground. In 1978, along with other underground writers, he published some of these poems together with more recent work on the Democracy Wall in Beijing, and in the unoffical literary magazine *Jintian* [Today]. After Deng Xiaoping's crackdown on the democratic movement in the spring of 1979, several of the younger writers drifted towards the official press, and poems by Bei Dao and his friends began to appear in national and provincial literary magazines.[3] Bei Dao's first officially published poem appeared in *Shikan* [Poetry] in 1979; the next year, 13 poems appeared in print; in 1981, 11; in 1982, 11 again; in 1983, only one batch of 3 (in an obscure journal from Kunming); in 1984, 7 (all in the second half of the year). With his reputation, Bei Dao was even in these early years usually responding to requests for contributions rather than submitting work for consideration, and it was clear that in 1983 and

[1] For instance, it is not clear whether the deletions and other alterations are marked on the manuscript itself or are inferred by a comparison between both versions.

[2] What King calls 'of the "It was a dark and stormy night" variety.'

[3] See McDougall, 'Breaking Through: Literature and the Arts in China, 1976–1986', *Copenhagen Papers in East and Southeast Asian Studies*, no. 1, 1988, pp. 35–65.

up until the summer of the following year, he was blacklisted from the literary journals that had previously solicited his work.

The existence of blacklisting was confirmed during the mid 1980s as copies of a restricted-circulation bulletin by the name of *Xuanchuan Dongtai* [Propaganda Trends] became available to Western journalists and scholars. Referring more widely than purely literary matters, they included such details as names of writers to be excluded as well as guidance on topics to be avoided or encouraged. Western observers have long taken for granted the systemic nature of censorship and propaganda in China, although the nature of the administrative structure was until recently obscure. Nevertheless, while the basic fact of censorship has hardly been questioned, too many journalistic and scholarly accounts of China since 1949, including almost all literary studies, simply ignore the operation of censorship (or even propaganda): the contrast with informed journalism and scholarship on Eastern Europe is striking.[1] Even Andrew Nathan's *Chinese Democracy*,[2] the most comprehensive account to date of the formal and informal operation of propaganda and censorship, is elusive on detail.

One aspect of Chinese censorship that is particularly difficult to quantify is its system of active incentives in addition to the better-known disincentives. The violent persecution of writers in China is certainly well-established. Mao Zedong once claimed that writers were not executed by the Communist Party as they had been by the Nationalists: the only exception had been Wang Shiwei, in the peculiar circumstances of war.[3] It is true that writers arrested in the early years after the establishment of Communist Party rule like Hu Feng and Lu Ling were not executed, but their privations leading to early death should certainly be regarded as belonging in the same category as Wang Shiwei's fate.

---

[1] Apart from the scholarly works cited above in footnote 2, see also the useful notes on censorship and self-censorship in Timothy Garton Ash, *The Uses of Adversity: Essays on the Fate of Central Europe* (Vintage Books, New York 1989).

[2] Andrew J. Nathan, *Chinese Democracy* (University of California Press, Berkeley 1985); see especially Chapter 7, 'The Media in the Service of the State', pp. 152–171. A useful background introduction to the early 1980s is given in the introduction to Perry Link, ed., *Stubborn Weeds: Popular and Controversial Chinese Literature after the Cultural Revolution* (Indiana University Press, Bloomington 1983); it lacks details of the administrative operation of censorship, however.

[3] For a brief account of the circumstances leading up to Wang Shiwei's execution in 1947, see Gregor Benton, 'Writers and the Party: The Ordeal of Wang Shiwei, Yanan, 1942' in Benton, ed., *Wild Lilies: Poisonous Weeds, Dissident Voices from People's China* (Pluto Press, London 1982), pp. 168–75.

At the time of the execution of five young Communist writers by the Nationalists in 1931, the Nationalists claimed that these young men were punished not for their literary efforts but for their participation in conspiracies to overthrow the government by force. Since writing and writers are so heavily politicised in China, the distinction between political struggles and literary persecution is by no means a simple matter. In post-1949 China, for instance, it can be said with equal force that Ding Ling's humiliation in the Anti-Rightist campaign of the late 1950s was a result of her active participation in factional politics on what turned out to be the losing side, rather than punishment as a writer for her literary activities; and when her faction regained power after the Cultural Revolution, she was restored to play an active role in politics again — see, for example, her participation in the persecution of younger writers in the Spiritual Pollution campaign of the early 1980s.

It might have been thought that the severity of punishment given to writers like Ding Ling and Ai Qing in the Anti-Rightist campaign and again in the early years of the Cultural Revolution might have deterred anyone from adopting a literary career, especially as the factional struggles on the literary front continued past the early Cultural Revolution years. On the contrary, when publication of literary works was resumed in the early 1970s, there seems to have been no shortage of manuscripts offered by or solicited from both established and newer writers.[1] Writers still formally blacklisted were permitted to use pseudonyms or pretend that their work was a 'collective' effort,[2] but had it run into trouble, their nominal pretence at anonymity would not have helped them evade punishment. No-one, after all, is literally obliged to write in order to live: to send a manuscript off to a publisher is always a matter of deliberate choice,[3] and in China, where unemployment was effectively non-existent before the Cultural Revolution, literary writing as a first choice for basic livelihood was simply not an available option.

[1] For a brief account of literary publishing during the Cultural Revolution see McDougall, 'Poems, Poets, and *Poetry* 1976: An Exercise in the Typology of Modern Chinese Literature', *Contemporary China*, vol. 2 no. 4 (Winter 1978), pp. 76–124.

[2] See for example testimony given by Qin Zhaoyang on his Cultural Revolution years in Richard King, '"Rightist" in the Wilderness: Qin Zhaoyang's Memories of His Twenty Years of Ostracism', *Modern Chinese Literature Newsletter*, vol. 6 no. 2 (Fall 1980), pp. 11–20.

[3] Chinese writers, like their Western counterparts, are sometimes cagey on this point, claiming, for instance, that a 'friend' sent their manuscripts (particularly the first one) to a publisher or literary agent.

When disincentives towards a literary career are so strong, the positive incentives must be at least equally strong. Even amateurs could usefully enhance their income with writing paid on the basis of a set fee per number of
words, and in a poverty-stricken country like China, the meagre remu-
nerations at the bottom of the literary ladder were attractive. Again, it is
very difficult to say which of the several kinds and amounts of rewards that
writers receive in China are due to them as participants in the propaganda
machine and which are due to them as writers. The basic rewards to
recognised professional writers, such as guaranteed regular salaries, employment, housing, health care and paid vacation leave, may be regarded as
a fair return on effort and talent, and many Chinese writers are still, even
today, reluctant to abandon economic security for the kind of freedom that
entails risk of destitution or forced change of occupation in the case of
failure in the literary marketplace.

At the top of the literary ladder, not only are the material rewards more
substantial but the immaterial rewards — the status indicating social ac-
ceptance, the power of control over their own lives and others' — are to
some writers even more seductive than higher salaries and better housing.
For some, it could be as simple as a sense of belonging. In a short article
about the Christa Wolf affair, Wolf Bierman recounts an incident when
Honecker's wife visited him to try to perusade him to become more orthodox, talking to him somewhat in the manner of a mother exhorting her
son to do better at school (I know you could, if you just tried...): 'And
that's how we talked to one another: yes, we were enemies, enemies down
the last breath; but we were family.'[1]

The same 'family atmosphere' permeated the Chinese literary world, of
which the dissident writers were a part: on the fringes, perhaps, but with
access to the centre. A description is found in Bei Dao's 'Gaozhishangde
yueliang' [Moon on the manuscript] of the relationship between writer and
literary bureaucrat (i.e. old ex-writer): the younger writer in this case is not
portrayed as a dissident, but the account corresponds to my own observations of dissidents in familiar social encounters with literary officials.[2]

[1] Wolf Bierman, 'Family Arguments', *Granta*, no. 35 (Spring 1991), pp. 233–42, esp.
p. 240. Christa Wolf's 'What Remains', first published in English in *Granta*, no. 33
(Summer 1990), describes her experience of being watched and followed by Stasi agents;
it has been at the centre of a controversy about East German writers and their
relationship to the State.
[2] For the English translation, see Bei Dao, *Waves*, (New Directions, New York1990),
pp. 41–52. See also the general process of assimilation described in McDougall,
'Breaking Through' op. cit.

It is hardly surprising, therefore, that the most pervasive form that censorship takes in post–1949 Chinese writing is self-censorship, not just as a sub-variety of general socialisation but as a reaction to the very powerful and specific inducements of rewards in status, power and material gain. The internalising of the régime's values, so strikingly evidenced in Guo Moruo during the Cultural Revolution or the post-Cultural Revolution Ai Qing, is more likely to be a product of immaterial rewards. Hilary Chung has produced an excellent case-study of self-censorship in a literary context by one of the regime's most powerful literary figures, Mao Dun:[1] if this living relic of an earlier age still felt obliged in 1980/81 to censor his autobiographical account of incidents that happened half a century ago for reasons of political discretion or prudery, it is hardly likely that he did so for the sake of an immediate improvement in his material welfare or for fear of brutal punishment.

It would be a mistake to think of this process of internalisation as brain-washing; as indicated by Liang Congjie, self-censorship is pre-eminently a perfectly rational reaction, in terms of an individual's short-term interests, to any system of rewards and punishments. It is widely practised at all times and in all countries, and is more pronounced to the extent that the system itself is more threatening (as in contemporary China). Miklós Haraszti's *The Velvet Prison*, a heavily ironic account of self-censorship practised by writers and artists in Hungary (first published in France in 1983), fails to grasp the simple point that rational decisions based on self-interest are the easiest to adjust when conditions change. In portraying Hungarian writers and artists as suffering from an irreversible form of brain-rot, he failed to see that the Eastern European societies were in the very process of undergoing the kind of fundamental change that his thesis claimed was impossible.[2]

---

[1] See Hilary Chung, 'The Portrayal of Women in Mao Dun's Early Fiction 1927–1932', PhD. thesis, Durham University, 1992, pp. 8–10 and passim. The reference is to vol. 1 of Mao Dun's *Wo zouguode lu* [The path I've travelled], published in 1981, compared with his 'Ji ju jiu hua' [Remarks on the past], written in 1933, and with 'Cong Guling dao Dongjing' [From Guling to Tokyo], published in 1928.

[2] See also 'The Carrot or the Stick' by Richard Aczel, a review of *The Velvet Prison* in *The Times Literary Supplement*, 2nd September, 1988, p. 956. In a paper given in 1990, I noted that the 'velvet prison' thesis had proved itself demonstrably invalid. Unfortunately, in the printed summary of this paper, 'invalid' was printed as 'valid', and I take this opportunity to correct the record; see McDougall, 'The Creation of Canons in Contemporary Chinese Literature', *Bulletin of the British Association for Chinese Studies*, 1990, pp. 13–15.

CENSORSHIP, SELF-CENSORSHIP AND LITERARY VALUES

To return to the point made by Birch above, it is by no means to be taken for granted that censorship or self-censorship inevitably guarantees poor writing. Timothy Garton Ash comments that in the Eastern European countries, the limitations of censorship, 'like the limitations of traditional forms — the sonnet or ballad — can have artistic advantages'; later, noting how Havel's work for the stage was 'deformed and diminished by censorship and persecution', he immediately adds, 'If he were a poet, it might be different.'[1] I have suggested above that it is at least theoretically possible to argue that the shrillness and relentless hammering home of the writer's point of view that are so endemic in Chinese writing make the removal of some of the passages critical of Party policy in Zhu Lin's story an improvement. For a more concrete analysis of the literary effects of self-censorship, I should like to compare two short stories written and published in 1977–78: 'Banzhu ren' [The class teacher][2] by Liu Xinwu (b. 1942) and 'Zai feixushang' [In the ruins][3] by Bei Dao (b. 1949). Both stories deal with education and the fate of teachers during the Cultural Revolution, at that time a very sensitive issue, and both temper their criticism of the past and the immediate present, presumably for entirely understandable reasons of personal security: literary factionalism and politics were still very tense in the immediate aftermath of the Cultural Revolution.

Liu Xinwu's career has been remarkable. From an early start as a hack writer in the 1960s, he achieved considerable fame for leading the new literary troops in the late 1970s, unexpectedly developed a powerful individual voice in the middle 1980s and ended the decade in official disgrace for having allowed publication of a short story in 1987 which was at once condemned as unacceptable. The machinations behind the writing and publication of 'The Class Teacher' may never be wholly transparent, but it seems clear that he was given the nod to venture into one patch of what was formerly forbidden territory. At the same time, the possible consequences of a miscalculation (whether his or others') in the current political mood also counselled caution — this need hardly be underlined.

One of the major breakthroughs in Liu Xinwu's story is his choice of an intellectual as protagonist. One could argue that this is unavoidable in a story

[1] Timothy Garton Ash, op. cit., pp. 16 & 169.
[2] For one of several English translations, see *Prize-Winning Stories from China, 1978–1979*, (Foreign Languages Press, Beijing 1981), pp. 3–26.
[3] For the English translation, see Bei Dao, *Waves*, op. cit., pp. 1–8.

dealing with education, but it was certainly daring to present as hero a schoolteacher of blatantly intellectual inclinations, Zhang Junshi, who is not specifically identified as coming from a proletarian background and who does not at any stage in the story make a serious mistake in judgement and confess his error before the masses, to be absolved by a kindly old Party cadre of worker/peasant/soldier origin. Underlining his innovative characterisation, Liu Xinwu also gave a leading role to a young ultra-leftist of working-class origin, Xie Huimin, the young secretary of the class Youth League branch: since there was not yet an accepted 'model' for a Gang of Four supporter, he was treading shaky ground here. As if in compensation for this daring, however, the story begins and ends with the inevitable invocation of Party authority, in the person of 'the tanned and fit Old Cao, Party Secretary of Guangming Middle School', for approval of the teacher's actions. Even more obtrusive are editorializings such as '[the young delinquent] was lucky to be part of a society where there was sufficient food and clothing', a comment that is not only false but also entirely unnecessary to plot, atmosphere or characterisation (self-censorship can be as much a matter of adding falsehoods as suppressing the truth). The brightly optimistic ending is similarly conventional, and expressed moreover in an ineffably trite and tinny formula: 'The sweet fragrance of flowers and the twinking stars overhead seemed to offer approval and encouragement...'. Liu Xinwu's use of a semi-autobiographical alter ego is here a tedious device for winning approval for both character and author and reducing to a minimum the ambiguity inherent in fiction.

Bei Dao's story was written for publication in *Today*. He had full editorial control (it is unlikely that his co-editor exerted any pressure on him), and since the magazine was outside the state apparatus, he was free from bureaucratic intervention. In one way, however, he was more constricted than in his underground days. Then, any unauthorised work brought so much risk to the author that although caution in expression was still advisable, one might just as well be hung for a sheep. In the short period when 'unofficial' publications flourished, however, although the authorities were less intolerant, they were also less remote, so that discretion became more pressing.

The protagonist of 'In the Ruins' is a professor at Beijing University who has been summoned by Red Guards to confess his errors; his decision to commit suicide rather than face certain humiliation, however, is set aside after an encounter with a young girl from a local peasant family who has also suffered in the Cultural Revolution. One line in the narrative (where the hero defends his books which have been under attack for years) could be read as a negative reference to the pre-Cultural Revolution period, which at that time was still outside the realm of permitted criticism, but elsewhere there is no more denunciation of either the pre-Cultural Revolution past or the post-Cultural Revolution present than there is in 'The Class Teacher': both authors are equally careful in this respect.

Bei Dao, however, avoids the self-censorship in commission practised by Liu Xinwu. His intellectual hero, for instance, is not glamorized as is Liu Xinwu's, who in this respect follows the orthodoxy of presenting unflawed heros; Bei Dao's hero, on the other hand, is flawed in the Lu Xun rather than the Jiang Qing mode prescribed for intellectuals. Bei Dao also avoids an outright condemnation of the Red Guard accuser, the professor even imagining his eventual repentance. Each thought or reflection in the story is firmly linked to the actual circumstances of the protagonist (who shows no sign of identity with the author), in distinction to Liu Xinwu's disingenuous manipulation of his alter ego's voice. In the context of Chinese fiction at that time, Bei Dao's ending is anything but orthodox (an empty noose swinging in the wind), though it might be thought visually banal. Finally, while Liu Xinwu's story belabours a simple message of victory for the side now in power, Bei Dao's suggests a complex inter-relationship of time, history and identity in which there are no winners.

To sum up, in 'The Class Teacher', self-censorship restricts the boundaries of the writer's imagination and coarsens his style, whereas in 'In the Ruins', it contrives a textual subtlety that allows multiple interpretations; for example, the Red Guard as the story's true protagonist.[1]

In the troubled conditions of the first half of the century, censorship and self-censorship also influenced literary writing, although generally to less devastating effect (censorship then was neither as intolerant nor as far-reaching as in the following forty years). Two examples of self-censorship in fiction from the 1930s are Lao She's 'Hei-bai Li' [Black Li and White Li], written in 1931–34 and published in 1943,[2] and Xiao Qian's 'Daopang' [At the side of the road], written in 1935 and published in 1936 in the

[1] For an analysis of ambiguities in 'In the Ruins', see McDougall, 'Zhao Zhenkai's Fiction: A Study in Cultural Alienation', *Modern Chinese Literature*, vol. 1 no. 1 (September 1984), pp. 103–30.
[2] For a commentary together with one of several English versions, see Leo Ou-fan Lee, 'Lao She's "Black Li and White Li": A Reading in Psychological Structure', in Theodore Huters, ed., *Reading the Modern Chinese Short Story* (M. E. Sharpe, Armonk 1990), pp. 22–36, and the translation on pp. 121–36.

collection *Lixia ji* [Under the fence].[1] Lao She later claimed that it was for fear of censorship that he dared not openly describe how White Li joined a Communist organiszation;[2] Xiao Qian's story similarly suppressed an overt reference to the growing threat of Japanese invasion, the true theme of the story.[3] In both cases, it seems to me that the stories gained in depth and universality as a result of their authors' entirely understandable discretion. The terse bleakness of Lu Xun's short stories and prose poems can also be attributed in part to self-censorship under a repressive regime.

I should like to stress that I am not in any sense defending the institutions of political censorship in China. What I do wish to point out is that it is naive to place the whole blame on censorship or even actual literary persecution for the intellectual and artistic poverty of China in the last forty years.

CONCLUSION

What Chinese readers want to read, and what Chinese writers want to write, is a literature of sex, love and dreams — as everywhere else in the world. Censorship distorts the relationship between writers and readers by throwing an unnatural emphasis on the importance of writers, the written word, and the political uses of literature. Under censorship, the writer is obliged to choose between the roles of official spokesman, moderate reformer or dissident. Censorship, especially post-1949 censorship, did not create the obsession of Chinese writers with China's fate (or, more precisely, the obsession of Chinese writers with the fate of Chinese intellectuals), but it reinforced it.

Censorship also upsets the balance between different kinds of writing: experimental, crusading, cathartic, entertaining, uplifting, soothing. One of the worst effects of censorship, from the point of view of the reader, is not simple prohibition or limitation, but the dissemination of the orthodox, the banal and the third-rate. The effects are felt not just in individual works but in a general climate that deters some writers and some works and encourages others, for instance, through active recruitment by the authorities to the literary professions which in turn give access to the channels

---

[1] Not translated into English. For a brief comment by this author, see Zbigniew Slupski, ed., *A Selective Guide to Chinese Literature 1900–1949, Volume 2 The Short Story* (Brill, Leiden 1988), pp. 212–13.

[2] Quoted by Leo Ou-fan Lee, op. cit., p. 32.

[3] Xiao Qian elaborated on the 'hidden meaning' of the story to this author in preparation for the entries on his short stories in A *Selective Guide,* op. cit.

for creative output.[1] People with the talent and ability to create a more impressive kind of literary output might plausibly be more frightened off by the dangers than attracted by the rewards of a system as described above, while the more opportunistic and less imaginative may be so lured by the rewards as to disregard the consequences of failure to keep abreast of political change.

Liu Binyan, describing Guo Moruo as 'shameless' and Shen Congwen as 'smart',[2] could at the same time have commented on the relative literary intelligence of the two writers: the Chinese reader has had to bear the effusions of the former and the silence of the latter when the contrary might have prevailed in a different structure of literary management and economics. The Chinese reader might seriously ask whether it would be better to have nothing at all rather than the official products of post-1949 literature, and regard the people who wrote them as having committed serious offences against their own people and their culture.

As for the future, I do not expect that Chinese intellectuals (including writers) will revert so easily to the practices of the first thirty years of Communist Party rule. The implicit bargain between the intellectual élite and the political élite, which worked moderately well in the 1950s, persisted (paradoxically) during the Cultural Revolution when both fell from power, and flourished through the greater part of the 1980s, has since 1987 been discredited.[3] The June 4th Massacre of 1989 drastically widened the gulf between intellectuals and the government, but also for the first time in many decades, gave to intellectuals a sense of common cause with the general population of the bigger towns and cities. Chinese intellectuals may now have regained what they have not possessed since the war against Japan: a wish and an ability to address their natural readers and not their usual secondary audience of censoring literary bureaucrats.

---

[1] I am grateful to Göran Sommardal for his discussion of these issues at the conference and in subsequent correspondence.

[2] Liu Binyan, *China's Crisis, China's Hope*, op. cit., p. 38.

[3] ibid. pp. 137–39, also McDougall, 'Breaking Through', op. cit., pp. 60–61.

REPORTING THE UNWANTED: CHINESE PRESS COVERAGE OF THE CZECHOSLOVAK VELVET REVOLUTION

LUCIE BOROTA

THIS PAPER CONCERNS the coverage of the Czechoslovakian Velvet Revolution in *Renmin Ribao* [People's Daily], the official party paper in the People's Republic of China (PRC). *Renmin Ribao* is theoretically accessible to everyone in the PRC and it has a more extensive coverage of foreign news than other mass media papers in China.

The name 'Velvet Revolution' has been given to the ten days of non-violent demonstrations in Prague and other cities in Czechoslovakia which culminated in a nationwide strike on November 27th 1989. As a result of the strike the Communist government and the president resigned. A new, non-communist government was formed and Vaclav Havel, the dissident leader, was elected president.

To make it easier to follow the *Renmin Ribao* coverage it is necessary to spell out the main events of the Velvet Revolution. On the evening of November 17th there was a student demonstration which was encircled by police who beat up demonstrators. The next day the actors from the National Theatre went on strike and demonstrators gathered in Wenceslas Square in the centre of Prague. On November 19th dissidents formed a political group called Civic Forum. University students from five major cities went on strike the following day.

The number of demonstrators in Wenceslas Square increased each day until there were around 300,000 people. On 24th November the Party Secretary Jakes resigned at a specially held session of the Central Committee. There was no factual coverage of these events in the official Czechoslovakian media until November 25th when the new secretary of the Communist Party called for a dialogue with Civic Forum.

The following day, Sunday November 26th, over a million people demonstrating in Letna Park were addressed by Havel and Dubcek, the leading politician in the events of 1968 Prague Spring. There was a general strike on Monday in which 80% of the workers participated. This was the turning point of the events: from this time on the Czechoslovakian Communist Party had effectively lost its authority.

On November 28th and 29th the government agreed to a number of concessions which included renouncing the automatic right of the Communist Party to govern the country. A new government was formed on December 3rd but 75% of its members were still communists and this incited further protests and demonstrations. On December 7th after the Prime Minister's resignation, the newly nominated Prime Minister Calfa turned his back on President Husak, formed a non-Communist government and eventually resigned his membership of the Party. Husak resigned on December 10th and on December 29th Havel was elected President of Czechoslovakia. The events culminated in June 1990 when free elections were held which confirmed the trend of political development and successfully concluded the Velvet Revolution.

To turn now to the reporting of these events in *Renmin Ribao*. The coverage can be summed up by saying that the more radical the political changes the less was reported about them. Moreover, the reports in *Renmin Ribao* always post-dated the events they covered by about three days. For example, the coverage on November 23rd was based on a telex transmitted on the 20th. At best, an article on the 28th, based on a telex from the 27th, reported on events from the previous day. The first mention of unrest in Prague was made on November 23rd and this was based on two telexes of November 20th and 21st.

In order to illustrate the nature of the coverage I shall consider this article of November 23rd in some detail. The main part of it concerned the meeting of the Czechoslovak government in Prague on November 20th, which had resulted in an uninformative communique. Parotting the words of this communique the article said that, in accordance with the Constitution, the socialist system in Czechoslovakia must be protected. Forces which disrupt order can only benefit counter-revolutionaries, and are against the interests of the people. One of the two direct quotations from the communique said: 'The government is against bloodshed and does not want any clashes. However, the government cannot tolerate the breaking of the constitutional law.'

The editors of *Renmin Ribao* therefore chose to highlight that section of the communique which threatened violent confrontations with the demonstrators — for this is how the quote should be understood — or which, in other words, agreed with its own policy.

A brief paragraph concluding the article read: 'Since November 17th there have been continuous demonstrations by mainly students and some other citizens in Prague. On the afternoon of the 30th there were more than 100,000 people in Wenceslas Square. According to the Czechoslovakian Press Agency their slogans were 'Pluralism', 'Free Elections', 'Thorough Reforms' etc. The demonstrations are not spreading to other cities.'

The article which appeared on November 25th, based on telexes of 22nd and 23rd, shared some of the same features. The main part consisted of a report by the Communist Party and the government, with *Renmin Ribao* concurring with the view expressed and again using quotations compatible with Chinese Communist Party policy. The only information about the actual events — the demonstrations and strikes — was contained in a short concluding paragraph. However, this information stood alone and without context; no background explanation was ever provided.

The use of information was selective. For example, the slogans mentioned above were the milder ones. The second article avoided giving the exact content of the slogans by reporting: 'Demonstrators shouted extreme (*jilie*) slogans.' This article also stated that the Prime Minister had met with student leaders and the recently established Civic Forum. This was the first mention of Civic Forum in *Renmin Ribao* but no attempt was made to explain its role as the main opposition force. Consequently, it is doubtful if the article made very much sense to the general Chinese readership. In the same article it was reported that Stepan, a member of the Central Committee, visited the workers of a steel plant to talk them out of joining the strike planned for November 27th. The report neglected to mention that Stepan was whistled down and left without being able to finish his speech. Furthermore this was the only mention of the general strike in *Renmin Ribao*.

The next two articles appeared on November 26th and 28th. Their approach was quite different. They concentrated on the proceedings of the special session of the Communist Party of Czechoslovakia to the exclusion of all other events. They therefore failed to report the first meeting between Civic Forum and the government. By this time the pre-eminent role of the Communist Party in Czechoslovakian politics had all but disappeared, a fact that the editors chose to ignore.

Articles in December indicate that the editors were aware that the Communist Party had been toppled, and it seems that once this fact had been recognized they chose to give only the most rudimentary coverage of events. There were eight articles about Czechoslovakia in the whole of

December of which three were devoted entirely to internal Communist Party affairs. The remaining five were rather different. Those of the 5th and 12th reported the change of government by stating how many members of each political party formed the new government. No individuals were named and there was no explanation of how or why these changes had occurred. On the 31st a short article in the bottom righthand corner of the front page reported Havel's election as President of the republic. This was the first time his name had been mentioned in China; although by this time his photograph had featured on the covers of political journals throughout the world. A biographical note stated: 'Vaclav Havel is 53 years old, a dramatist, one of the founding members of Charta 77, and an important representative of Civic Forum'. This information was given in isolation; there was no explanation of what Charta 77 was, no comment on Havel having been a dissident leader, his history of imprisonment or other information to put the event in context.

At the end of each year *Renmin Ribao* publishes lengthy analytical articles by prominent personalities. In the 'Special International Section' (*Guoji zhuan ye*) of the paper on December 23rd there was an article titled 'Reactions of Academics to International Politics'. It contained a paragraph on Eastern Europe although no country was mentioned specifically. It said, to paraphrase, that 'most academics believe that the turbulent situation in Eastern Europe should be coolly observed. It is hard to predict which direction it will take because there are too many internal and external factors playing a role, but that the final decision is for the people to make. So far reactionary forces have also appeared but those loyal to communism and socialism continue their active work and search for the correct reforms so that future development will not be led astray by certain peoples schemes... when considered in the long term the present changes are merely clashes between two rival systems (socialism and capitalism). From a historical perspective, even though capitalism may be revived a few times, or even develop for a few centuries, it will still eventually disintegrate into a permanent state of crisis.' The vagueness and omission of hard facts shown by this paraphrase are typical of such articles.

When speaking of late December 1989 we must bear in mind that all other events in Europe were overshadowed by those in Romania. A massacre of civilians in Timisoara had provoked an uprising which overthrew the government, and the two dictators were executed on December 25th. The other two long summaries of international politics in *Renmin Ribao* of this time presumably had these events in mind, although they did not refer to them directly. One of the articles was Li Peng's speech at the plenary meeting of the State Council published on December 28th. The other was by a Foreign Ministry spokesman, published the following day. Li Peng stated: 'No matter what happens in other countries, we will maintain the policy of non-interference in the internal affairs of other countries.' This was obviously a double-edged statement which referred as much to the worldwide reaction to the Tiananmen massacre as to Romanian events. Li Peng also noted that the works of Mao and Marx must be studied increasingly because capitalist ideology had been infecting cadres.

The other basic attitude found in China to the development in Eastern Europe is expressed in *Guangming Ribao*, another national daily paper in the PRC, where it was said that the changes were caused by Western capitalists and that China was the only country remaining to defend socialism. In 1990 the reports in *Renmin Ribao* fitted in with this approach. There were five articles in January, seven in February and three in March. They were all short and were concerned with Czechoslovak foreign policy as it related to a limited number of other countries and organizations (namely the two Germanies, USA, France, the European Parliament and the former Soviet Union). Reading the articles it seems as if these, rather than Czechoslovakia, were the main interest for *Renmin Ribao*.

Most of the articles in the first quarter of 1990 were about the withdrawal of the Soviet army from Czechoslovakia. The negotiations, movements of arms, numbers of soldiers and vehicles, and locations were all provided. The attention paid to this is not merely due to Chinese interest in the former Soviet Union, but it reveals the official Chinese presentation of the Velvet Revolution. It is not presented as the downfall of a Communist regime, but as the end of Soviet domination in Central and Eastern Europe. This view had been reinforced by the reactions of members of Chinese delegations to Czechoslovakia: while they expected to see economic changes, they were also expecting political continuity and were not prepared for Czechoslovakia's rejection of this.

The articles which appeared in 1990 about the Communist Party written in the old style, quoting Communist comrades in Czechoslovakia should also be understood in this light. The articles of February 19th concerned the expulsion of party leaders, among them President Husak and Prime Minister Strougal, and although it gives their names it does not give their official positions. There is also a quote from the new Chairman of the Party: 'There were also good things done in the past and good men deserve praise.' This is a double-edged statement. The speaker was probably hinting at the accepted evaluation of Mao Zedong, and a Chinese reader would immediately understand the allusion. The authorities in China now commonly assert that 70% of Mao's actions were good but the remaining 30% were wrong. In this way they avoid having to make a full criticism or appraisal.

On March 19th a slightly longer article appeared concerned with the election of a new Communist Party secretary and his complaints about criticisms raised against the Communist Party at that time. He said that in the light of these criticisms, the parliamentary elections in June would not be fair. The editors persistent focus on the Communist Party was inadequate to explain the real situation in Czechoslovakia. In June 1990, the elections finally successfully concluded the Velvet Revolution, and the restrained attitude of the Chinese press has remained unchanged.

Before concluding I would like to look briefly at three other factors relevant to this discussion. First, the coverage of Czechoslovakia in the *Renmin Ribao* while the Communists were still in power. At that time there were frequent articles on the international news page often also concerned with other countries also in the Soviet bloc. For example, there were seven articles in July 1989 although nothing of great significance was happening in Czechoslovakia. Four were on economic matters, one on education and two on international affairs (July 2nd about the expulsion of a US diplomat and July 3rd a report on a treaty signed with Poland and the GDR). In addition, about once a month, there was a feature article on the Special International Reports page. The feature carried on July 10th concerned the educational system, and there was a photograph of a Prague school in the next day. Ironically enough, on the first day of the Velvet Revolution there was a feature article on the Prague underground railway.

Secondly, it is interesting to consider the official stand of the Czechoslovakian government towards the democracy movement in PRC. Cuba, Czechoslovakia and GDR were the first countries to express their approval of the Tiananmen massacre. On Czechoslovakian television there was a shot of the student demonstrations in May, and in late June and July there were two items on the trials in China, but the massacre was ignored. The official Chinese version of events was given in the press. After the Velvet Revolution this attitude changed and several events took place in Czechoslovakia which were not agreeable to the Chinese government: the student protests against June 4th in front of the Chinese Embassy in Prague; the visit of the Dalai Lama to Prague in 1990; Mrs Havel's visit to Taiwan in 1991; and repeated critical articles in the press. However, these were all unofficial. The official statement given by the Foreign Ministry on February 27th 1990 read: 'in stablilizing the new Czechoslovak foreign policy, our relations with the PRC play a significant role. Therefore

Czechoslovakia fully endorses the attitude of non-interference in the internal affairs of other countries and is interested in developing further its relations with the PRC.' This shows a cautious approach which is very much a legacy of the previous regime, a fear that any criticism may be punished by reductions in mutual trade.

The third consideration is the reception of the Velvet Revolution in the Taiwanese press. Even for a country with a vital interest in anything anti-communist, the coverage was quite extraordinary. From November 18th to the beginning of January there were almost daily front page stories accompanied by colour photographs. There was also a great deal of spontaneous interest among the Taiwanese people, who are generally interested, for obvious reasons, in small countries struggling for sovereignty.

In conclusion, it is clear that the Czechoslovak Velvet Revolution was a sensitive issue for the Chinese government coming only six months after Tiananmen. It received some coverage in *Renmin Ribao*, especially when compared with total silence of the Czechoslovak press over the Tiananmen massacre, but although it was possible to deduce the essentials from the reports it required considerable effort, because the facts appeared disjointedly without any introduction or background. The coverage of facts politically disagreeable to the Chinese government were presented so as to confuse rather than to inform and a reader without some prior knowledge would find it difficult to make sense of these reports.

It should however be noted that the Chinese people may have other sources of foreign news. The main ones are the foreign radio stations, such as the BBC and the Voice of America, and the weekly magazines restricted to specialists and party members, *Cankao xiaoxi* and *Cankao ziliao*. For those able to gain their background information from these sources the coverage in the *Renmin Ribao* provides guidance on the correct political stance to adopt towards the events. However, I am sceptical about the number of Chinese who have access to these other sources and believe that even among those who do, many may have become politically apathetic.

In general the reporting during the Velvet Revolution suffered because of the two to three days delay. It was distorted by favouring the Communist Party. Since the Communist Party soon became obsolete the reports were of little use. This was probably not a mistake in interpretation of the events but an intentional distortion. The editors of *Renmin Ribao* were direct and well informed. The Chinese Embassy in Prague has a remarkable number of staff fluent in Czech and they say their movements were not restricted.

There were also two journalists in Prague also fluent in Czech and at least one of them went to all of the November 1989 demonstrations.

The interesting feature of the coverage is how it changed. The first week it covered the activities of both the Communist regime and the demonstrators while concentrating on the former. Thereafter there was a period when it only carried stories on the Communist Party. Finally, after the downfall of the communist regime (which has never been openly acknowledged by *Renmin Ribao*), news about Czechoslovakia has been sparse and in many cases it has only been mentioned in articles with a different central issue. The former 'special treatment' of Czechoslovakia on the pages of *Renmin Ribao* was reserved for socialist countries only and has therefore disappeared with the old regime.

CHINA,
EASTERN EUROPE
AND THE FORMER
SOVIET UNION

CHINA, THE FORMER SOVIET UNION AND EASTERN EUROPE: SOME PRELIMINARY THOUGHTS

LIU BINYAN*

IT IS VERY DIFFICULT to compare China with the former Soviet Union and the countries of Eastern Europe; the political system is probably the only item common to them all. Also while events in Eastern Europe and the former Soviet Union have had an influence on events in China, the relation has not always been straightforward. For example, the reputation of the Communist Party (CP) inside China reached a peak during the time of Prague Spring in 1968, and revolutionary events in Eastern Europe, such as the workers' uprisings in 1953 in Berlin and 1956 in Poland, have sometimes led to reactionary events in China which have impeded the process of change.

One of the reasons that Mao initiated the Anti-Rightist Campaign in 1957, for example, was in reaction to the 1956 Hungarian uprising. He boasted that this counter-revolutionary event in Hungary had encouraged many small counter-revolutionary events in China which he was therefore able to suppress all in one go. The establishment of Solidarity in August 1980 was enthusiastically covered by the Chinese newspapers because the Chinese authorities judged the Polish government to be revisionist. But coverage of events ceased completely within a few months when they realised there could be a Polish-style movement in China which would inevitably damage the government. Only a few months before Solidarity was formed Deng Xiaoping had made a speech in which he said that there was a need for political reform in China; after Solidarity political reform was permanently postponed.

Among the many differences between China and Eastern Europe and the former Soviet Union, a crucial one is that of the relationship between the CP and the people. There is a special relationship between the Chinese people and the CP: simply put, the Chinese people sacrifice their freedom in return for a subsistence. In 1949 the majority of the Chinese did not feel that there was anything wrong with this as they did not then understand

* Translated by Wang Hao and Susan Whitfield.

the price they would have to pay for their lack of freedom. But within a few years they started to realise that not only were they without freedom, but even their basic existence was threatened.

First, the peasants were confronted with the famine in the countryside of 1953. In 1956 the workers started to feel dissatisfied as a result of the high inflation and low wages. The extent of the famine of the early 1960s — the largest man-made famine in China, with 30–40 million people dead — was only revealed to a few hundred people in China.

How do the Chinese react to this kind of event? The majority of them are either pessimistic and accepting, or respond with passive protest. When I was in the countryside from 1959–1978 the peasants simply stopped working; this was also the response of the workers during the Cultural Revolution, while the early 1980s saw the start of strikes among the workers. Another way of coping is to show lack of respect for the system by stealing, always from the public and not the private sector of course. There are even a few intellectuals who have continued political resistance over the past 40 years but they are always exposed very quickly and severely punished.

Another aspect of the relation between the people and the CP is that for the thirty year period between 1949 and 1979 the Chinese authorities did not need a secret service like the KGB because the Chinese people volunteered themselves as informers. While Maoism became bankrupt as a result of the Cultural Revolution, communist ideology remained deeply lodged in people's minds. And although it is now widespread for people to criticize and express their hatred of the CP. If you stand beside someone and shout 'Down with the CCP' then they will react immediately by calling you a counter-revolutionary.

Political reform in China lagged behind that in the former Soviet Union and Eastern Europe. One crucial reason for this is that none of the Chinese resistance movements of the last forty years have left a permanent impression: they have been forgotten by the people very quickly. Two aspects of the Chinese environment have had a setback effect on these movements. First, every political movement between 1949 and 1966, apart from the 1953 'Three-Anti' and the 1964 'Four-Clean' campaigns, was targeted at intellectuals, and intellectuals did not dare to stand up against these movements because in each case the workers, peasants and ordinary Chinese were on the government's side.

Another reason, however, is the natural weakness of Chinese intellectuals. For example, although Guo Moruo was well-known for rebelling against the Guomindang of Chiang Kai-Shek in his youth, in later life he became a devout disciple of the CP. Mao Dun's situation was very similar; he never openly criticised the CP, and he even wrote a letter, only recently discovered, requesting posthumous recognition as a CP member. Before 1949 Lao She was the most prolific writer in support of the CP but he committed suicide during the Cultural Revolution. Not many people understand why he died. In 1966 at the start of Cultural Revolution he was tortured and humiliated by the Red Guards, while other intellectuals such as Guo Moruo and Mao Dun were being protected by the CP. I suspect Lao She committed suicide because he felt the CP had treated him badly in comparison with these two and others.

While there are exceptions, many intellectuals are easily bribed by the government, but not for money. In fact, Chinese intellectuals have a higher regard for titles and reputation than for money, therefore if they are named as 'Representative of the National People's Congress', for example, they are afraid of losing the title and the honour it bestows. The obsession with titles is even shown by the namecards of Chinese writers, on which membership of their local writers' association or other organization is always noted along with a seat on the executive or any other position. This attitude even applies to Chinese intellectuals who live abroad, including world renowned scientists. When a group of Nobel Prize winners wrote a letter to the Chinese authorities to protest at the June 4th massacre and saying that, as a result, they would not visit China, the four Chinese Nobel Prize-holding physicists all refused to add their names. Chinese intellectuals regard it as highly prestigious if they are received by a leader such as Deng Xiaoping or Zhao Ziyang, and they feel particularly honoured if they shake hands with these people. I have even known some intellectuals who have copied the newspaper reports and photographs of such meetings and had hundreds of copies distributed to their friends and relatives.

Given the considerable political influence of the former Soviet Union and Eastern Europe there is pitifully little understanding of these countries in China. One reason is the lack of information owing to the difficulty of getting anything published on these countries. However, it is not impossible to publish. I have appealed again and again in China for someone to write an introduction to the culture and the history of the former Soviet Union, but no-one has responded despite the fact that there are many Chinese who know Russian and have spent time there. There are three reasons for their reticence. First, it is more difficult to write something independently is than to translate someone else's work. Secondly, translating a novel will make more money than this type of introductory book. And thirdly, and this is the crucial reason, they are afraid. They argue that if they write something about the former Soviet Union, in ten or twenty years when there is a new political movement in China they may be punished on account of this work. I would, however, respond to this third point by saying that the risk of punishment is in fact far smaller than their perceptions, perhaps only 1 in 10,000.

One attitude held by many intellectuals towards the limited intellectual freedom in China is exemplified by a recent conversation I had with a Chinese writer living in the USA. I argued that there have been very few intellectual uprisings in China compared to the former Soviet Union because China's intellectuals are afraid and submissive. He responded by saying that the Chinese situation was very different in that it was more difficult in China to act against the government. For example, he said, it is very difficult to publish samizdat because the paper supply is controlled by the government. I thought, although I did not say this at the time, that there is no need to buy paper in China because it is always possible to take it from your work unit, and you can also find friends who will take paper from their units to help you publish.

There are many other differences that make it difficult and of limited usefulness to compare the former Soviet Union and Eastern Europe with China. To begin with historical influence from the West is much more restricted in China: a Czechoslovakian's understanding of Western history and culture is probably much higher than my own. Also there is no democratic tradition in Chinese history and the cultural level is lower, with up to 25% illiteracy. And while the threat of the former Soviet Union generated considerable nationalist feelings in Eastern Europe which were important for their political development, the Sino-Soviet conflict had little effect on Chinese nationalism. Another difference is the lack of a strong religious community in China compared to the Catholic Church in Eastern European countries.

But, I would argue, one advantage that China has over the former Soviet Union and Eastern Europe is the experience of the ten year-long Cultural Revolution. which seriously wounded the body of the CP. Although it was initiated by Mao, it destroyed his ideology and his reputation among the Chinese people. Its most important outcome, however, was that it produced a whole new generation of Chinese people.

The people of China can be divided into four generations: those in their seventies and eighties; fifties and sixties; thirties and forties; and the younger Tiananmen Square generation. I believe that the most influential generation is the third — those in their thirties and forties — precisely because the majority of this generation have been through the Cultural Revolution. Initially many became Red Guards who were totally committed to Mao and in this role they committed many atrocities. Most later realised that their actions had been wrong and are now upset and repentant. Moreover, they have had a taste of democracy: at that time anyone could organize a group which could publish leaflets and give speeches: these could be called proto-political parties. Of course everyone still had to say that they supported Mao, but just like Westerners who say they support God, they could then do anything they wanted. Afterwards they became targets of Mao's political punishment and were sent to the countryside for periods of up to ten years, during which time they had the opportunity to understand the poverty and suffering of the Chinese peasant, and therefore they understand Chinese society better than any other age group.

From 1972 to the end of the decade, 200,000 of this generation entered university and now their members fill most of the regimental and divisional commanders in the People's Liberation Army. Compared to our older generation they have the character and courage to stand up, and the habit of thinking independently. Moreover, they are more mature than the younger, Tiananmen generation of Wuerkaixi and Chai Ling, and they have a better understanding of Chinese society. Among this generation are Wei Jingsheng, still in prison, and Wang Juntao and Chen Ziming, both sentenced in early 1991 to thirteen years imprisonment. Many more are middle-ranking officials in the Chinese bureaucracy and the most influential contemporary writers are all from this group; I could easily pick out twenty names as an illustration.

Also on the positive side, we must recognize that recently a minority of Chinese intellectuals have become braver and have dared to criticize the government, and we must also understand that even in Czechoslovakia, Vaclev Havel and other dissidents were a small minority. But I still maintain that intellectuals in China are weaker than those in Eastern Europe and the former Soviet Union.

Nor should we underestimate the impact of the 1989 movement. I believe there are now hundreds of underground political organizations operating in China. The official figure given by the State Security Bureau (*Anquan Bu*) is about seventy, with forty in Beijing, but I am sceptical about this total. If there are forty in Beijing alone, how can there be only thirty in the rest of the country? Also the Bureau acknowledges that there are underground workers' federations in five provinces ranging from Liaoning to Hunan, and there are also at least three underground newspapers in Beijing now and we can presume there are more elsewhere.

The youngest generation has also shown its worth. Some of those who were arrested because of their participation in the June 4th events have shown tremendous courage in continuing to speak out after their release. In some cases this has led to re-arrest, and the fact that some have been allowed to go abroad is not a sign of leniency on the part of the government, it is rather a means of preventing them causing further trouble in China. Gao Xing, one of the four hunger-strikers on Tiananmen in early June, is a typical example. When asked why he was sent abroad he said that he had met with foreign journalists more than 130 times and because the government was not able to stop him they sent him abroad. This kind of outspoken and persistent behaviour is rare among the intellectuals belonging to the first and second generation.

This is the situation now: as to what might happen next, I must say that although I am not very optimistic about China's future I am convinced the government will reform. I predict it will be forced to change from the inside under heavy pressure from forces within Chinese society as well as from foreign countries, although it will be prove difficult to overthrow. My feeling is that there are far fewer Chinese cadres against reform than there were Soviet cadres: for this reason, Gorbachev was unfortunate to be born in the former Soviet Union, he would have had far less trouble in initiating his reforms if he had been born in China!

If the government were to be overthrown, I am not optimistic about a China with political freedom. Hundreds of different political organizations would be bound to appear, resulting in instability. Finally, I always remind people that the major difficulty for China's future development is not to be found in the Japanese threat, the CP, or in Maoist ideology, but rather lies inside the minds of Chinese people. But this will have to be the subject of another paper.

Human Rights and the Reality of Appearances in Totalitarian China: A View from Moscow

Yuri Garushyants[*]

THE CONDITION OF HUMAN RIGHTS within the body politic is the best general indicator of the health of a society. By assessing the human rights situation in a society one thereby assesses its overall well-being. In the former Soviet Union, however, it was not only proponents of the prevailing ideology who resisted the idea that human rights are an independent part of a general humanitarian outlook. Those in opposition who called themselves socialists and supported a socialist path of development, were also slow to accept this idea. I saw myself how, during the Khrushchev period, there was hardly any development in attitudes among the intelligentsia on human rights issues (except perhaps among a narrow circle of lawyers), and no attempt was made to reach an understanding of the concept. And if it was mentioned in the press, which was wholly government controlled, then it was done so within quotation marks or qualified by the words 'so-called'.

The same situation has prevailed in China. While preparing this paper I reviewed several collections published in China in the second half of the 1950s marked 'for internal use only'. These consisted of excerpts of writings (comprising about two thousand pages) from the so-called 'right bourgeois' elements, that is, the participants in the opposition movement in China at that time (1957). No understanding of the concept of human rights is mainfested by these writings, and while the authors were grouped together according to thematic principles there was no rubric specifically for 'human rights'; all items which touched on this were classified under various other headings, such as 'Problems of co-operation in agriculture'.

The obvious explanation for the lack of understanding of the concept of human rights is the anti-human nature of 'concentration camp socialism' which has prevailed in China since 1949. But if we take this view a paradox arises. The idea of defending human rights was developed in precisely the period in which China was most isolated from the outside world and when its representative thinkers were living in exile in distant villages and

* Translated by Tamara Dragadze and Susan Whitfield.

mountain regions, or imprisoned in labour camps. During these two decades of bloodshed (counting from 1957, the Anti-Rightist Movement, and not from 1966, as is accepted in China), these thinkers were able to reach out beyond their suffering to the idea of defending human rights and, after the Gang of Four was isolated, they pursued this idea with some assurance. In my opinion, sinologists still have a lot of work to do to explain the phenomenon of this internally-driven change in attitudes.

The actions of Chinese human rights defenders exceeded all expectations from the start, although they turned out to be tragic for the organizers and active participants, who were arrested, brought to trial and received severe sentences. It was precisely this movement for the defence of human rights that became the unifying centre for all subsequent developments in the democratic opposition to China's regime, developments which reached their climax in the events of Tiananmen in the spring and early summer of 1989. At the same time all evaluations of the problems of human rights were produced by the same movement, despite the fact that realization of human rights based on such evaluations assumed the removal of the basic characteristics of the regime which had controlled China since 1949. In connection with this I shall dwell on one of the observations I have made in the course of my study.

Both in the former Soviet Union and in China (where I spent ten months from September 1989 to June 1990) the violence of Tiananmen was seen by many as a departure from the line taken by the Chinese leadership at the end of the 1970s and the beginning of the 1980s. This view was held even among democratically inclined circles and, incidentally, I have also heard it expressed by certain Western sinologists. Such a distorted view of the Chinese leadership is typical of thinkers in both the former Soviet Union and China, and can be explained by recognizing either that they are burdened with the dogmas of totalitarian thinking, or that they are hampered by an insufficient level of professionalism (although this does not account for the misperceptions by Western sinologists). In fact the political processes in China at the end of the 1970s and beginning of the 1980s, and those in 1989 are part of the same bitter narrative which, in my opinion, has still not been fully understood.

Right at the beginning of the last decade, or more precisely, on 25th January 1981 at the trial of the Gang of Four and others, the death sentence was passed on the Cultural Revolution. At the end of the same decade the organizers of this spiritually cleansing trial, carried out to provide an example to society, crushed with their tanks what by then had become a more mature Chinese democracy movement. Only at first appearance does the logic of the behaviour of the Chinese leadership on these two occasions seem to be contradictory. In fact, the act of the sentencing in January 1981 and the bloody reprisals of June 1989 were expressions of one and the same system of political thinking and of one and the same method of political action. The trial in January 1981 did not extend the death sentence to the totalitarian-terrorist regime, and if these actions are analysed within the framework of the different models adopted by China to achieve the 'socialist choice', it can be seen that neither departed from revolutionary-socialist rules.

Since 1949 China has tested three such models. The first was the Soviet model or, as it can also be called, the Stalinist model. This found fertile soil in China in the mid-1950s. It is characterized above all by commitment to the monopoly of the ruling party over all spheres of social and political life. That is, sole power is maintained by undivided rule in the army and a refined and all-embracing system of police control: a regime of 'totalitarian-terror'. National production, which was built on total socialization, was the excuse for centralization of authority through economic processes. Such an economic construct, which we fondly call today the 'command-economy', in practice blocked the realisation of the principle of 'pay according to one's work', and it resulted in employment often taking the character of forced labour. Another result was that such a totalitarian regime, fostered by the ideological concept of 'sharpening the class struggle under socialism', periodically turned to the annihilation of various social strata and groups in the community, usually as a preventive measure. In other words, ideas of political freedom and democracy had no influence on the reasoning of the founders of this society, and the spiritual flourishing of China's people was crushed by the heavy physical and moral loss of millions who were dragged into the socialist whirlpool. Individuality was to be sacrificed to the 'steel' constructions and 'iron and concrete' schema of Communist ideology which at this time (towards the mid-1950s) was untested in the former Soviet Union, in Eastern Europe or in China.

Based on the Soviet model, the regime of totalitarian-terror and the command economy immediately led to tangible failures in China: the flop of the first Five Year Plan; the destruction and impoverishment of the peasantry through mass co-operatives in the countryside (analogous to the collectivization of Soviet villages); and the disorganization of national production because of the curtailment of the already weak beginnings of the market. In the mid-1950s the totalitarian regime, directly copied from the Soviet model, passed through a phase of terror. I have in mind the unending campaigns of mass repressions after 1949. Analysis of these campaigns is difficult in the absence of reliable statistics, but according to *Renmin Ribao* (People's Daily) of September 10th, 1979, the Chinese courts had considered 8 to 9 million cases between October 1949 and May 1957 and only a third were criminal cases. In other words, there were 5 to 6 million cases of political dissent and, moreover, one case may have involved more than one, several hundred or even several thousand individuals. (Not included in these figures are the victims of Party and Communist Youth purges, or people who were dealt with within the framework of 'non-antagonistic contradictions within the people'). Even though the people represented by this figure were only a minority of the 400 million population of China at the time, the fact that this model was unacceptable for so many people in real terms suggests that it could hardly be considered socially just.

As the situation worsened the Chinese public began to react sensitively, prompted by the lessons of Hungary in 1956 and reports of the XXth Congress of the Communist Party of the Soviet Union denouncing the personality cult of Stalin. For the first time in Communist China in 1956 and 1957 an opposition was formed (the 'right bourgeois') which openly expressed its dissatisfaction with the regime's Soviet style of functioning. One indication that this expression was not limited to a few but had a mass character is the fact, now revealed in the official Chinese press, that over half a million people suffered repression during this period.[1]

In an attempt to soften the negative consequences of this first course and to confront opposition criticism, there was talk of the necessity for 'correcting' the 'classical model' (the model called 'leftist' in China today). In 1956 the question of the 'liberalisation' of the political and economic systems was discussed at the VIIIth Party Congress. Proposals included the removal of some administrative limits by re-organizing the system of government, espousing the doctrine of the 'hundred flowers', and allowing some elements of a market economy. All these steps were taken, it was stated, in order 'to perfect and strengthen socialism' which had apparently veered to the 'left': this was the reason for the various 'anomalies' and 'deformations' of the social and political processes in the country. In other words, there was no revision of the fundamental dogma of the Party on which the totalitarian structure of China was based: it was still claimed that socialism was the final goal, and the only mistake with the course taken by the government was that it had strayed temporarily from the correct path.

[1] Li Weihan, *Huiyi yu Yanjiu* (Reminisences and Research), vol. 2. (Zhongguo dangshi ziliao chubanshe, Beijing 1986), p. 871.

It is well known that at the same time, as a result of internal political struggles and through the personal initiative of Mao Zedong, the trend, albeit negligible, towards social healing was completely disrupted. From the mid-1960s, urged on by Mao himself, Chinese society began to function according to the Cultural Revolution model, which then came to replace the Soviet one. Here some people may protest that the Cultural Revolution model is identical to Stalin's 'totalitarian-terror' dictatorship, but I would reply that although the Cultural Revolution model genetically embraces the Stalinist model and they have many traits in common, they are not the same. The Cultural Revolution model is far narrower and went to absurd lengths as much through its methods of realisation (the role of the 'spontaneous' beginning, military control, the renouncing of the use of the active phase of terror of Party and Youth organizations, revolutionary committees and so on), as through its open proclamation of the goal of creating communism according to the pattern of life in an army barracks. The difference between these two models has even been noticed by Chinese authors, who call the latter 'ultra-leftist' in order to differentiate it from the 'leftist' Stalinist one.

At the beginning of the 1980s, having denounced the theory and practice of the Cultural Revolution by referring to it as the ragings of a 'feudal-fascist dictatorship', the ruling authorities headed by Deng Xiaoping re-animated the concept of 'the perfecting and strengthening of socialism' to provide the basis of a third model. Liu Shaoqi, Deng Xiaoping himself, and those who in contemporary China are counted as the old proletarian revolutionary guard had previously lost a struggle to have just such a model recognized. It differs from the previous two models in its reliance on less forceful methods of governing, less emphasis on destructive and more on constructive tasks, and the allowance of the development of market processes, albeit according to 'the socialist plan'. But as a working model it absorbed the fundamental political position of the previous two models, namely, to preserve (until the realization of the final goal of the utopian state) the dictatorship of 'class hegemony' through a one-party system of government ruling on a unified ideological and theoretical platform.

All three models fundamentally adhere to totalitarian-despotic values, lapidarily formulated in the Four Cardinal Principles attributed to Deng Xiaoping. They are: adherence to the socialist road, the dictatorship of the proletariat, the leadership of the Party, and the upholding of Marxist-Leninist-Mao Zedong Thought. At the end of the 1970s and beginning of the 1980s the democratic opposition resurrected itself after a twenty year interval, prompted by a renewed ideal of defending human rights. The

Party leaders immediately saw in the actions of this opposition the symptoms of a threat dangerous to themselves, in particular to both the basis and the superstructure of the State's institutions, just as with the opposition movement in the 1950s. By this time, however, the sentiments of social justice held by the Chinese opposition had been considerably sharpened by the tangible flaws of the concept of 'the perfection of socialism' and by the attempt to 'round the edges' of the policies of 'despotic socialism', which had brought the country to the brink of national catastrophe during the years of the Cultural Revolution. Independent thinking based on the experience of the previous three decades led China's opposition forces to develop a programme of protest, albeit of a negative character. The following are examples of declarations made in this programme.[1]

• The teachings of Marx and Lenin on class struggle do not coincide at all with the situation in contemporary China, nor with the teachings of Mao Zedong on classes and class struggle

• China has a government like the Soviet one but its main shortcoming is the limitless omnipotence of the authorities at a time when democracy is trampled on 'even more than in the USSR'

• the dictatorship of the proletariat is the root of all evil

• a regime should be established which corresponds to the national aspirations of China and appropriate reforms should be carried out

• establish a multi-party system as a counterbalance to the one-party state, to end the lack of a division between party and government which embodies the abandonment of building democracy

The same motives were, in one way or another, proclaimed in the demands of the democratic opposition of 1988 and 1989, and for this reason the activities of the Chinese authorities who ordered the army into Tiananmen Square was in no way a digression from the totalitarian methods accepted by China's rulers. Moreover, the death sentence passed on the Cultural Revolution in January 1981 and the bloody carnage carried out in June 1989 were both expressions of a unified system of political thinking and methods of political action. In neither case did the Chinese leadership introduce any modifications in its plan for building a utopian socialist society.

What can we expect 'to happen next?' In all likelihood the removal of 'scientific socialism' by China's people will take the whole of the next

[1] These are all taken from *Da zi bao* (Large character posters) posted in 1979.

decade, and they will have to have recourse to both national and international help. The outcome will depend greatly on how the situation develops in the former Soviet Union. The Soviet experience testifies that people parting with a totalitarian society have to pay a high price. The people of the former Soviet Union must overcome the resistance of the powerful conservative block, consisting mainly of the old party and the state bureaucracy, which for many years had the monopoly of the decision-making process in all spheres of social life. They must also get rid of the ideal of a social utopia: a process that will be especially tortuous for the millions of people with lumpen consciousness — the overwhelming lust for 'general equality'. In addition, the process is complicated by the fact that the dismantling of the old political system and economic structures following the general collapse of the socialist system, has been overtaken by processes of disintegration. The incredible rise in the people of a dying empire of a national consciousness has led to the government being on the verge of partial or even complete loss of administrative control and, as a result, there is a high level of social tension and political instability.

In two or three years it will probably be clear whether the peoples of the former Soviet Union — Russia first of all — have suceeded in constructing a democratic society, free of dictatorship and authoritarianism, and have been able to establish the rule of law and a socially oriented market economy. And it will also be clear how high a price has been paid for this first step toward civilized society. If they do succeed (and there is hope, even in Russia), then Chinese society (including some groups from the ruling elite) will insist more and more strongly insist on profound reforms, basing their demands on the heritage of the events of Tiananmen in 1989.

The collapse of the Chinese regime, in my opinion, will begin in the upper levels of power — as it did in the former Soviet Union — under pressure from opposition forces. It will be accompanied by the natural passing away of the Party gerontocracy, an intra-Party split and the resulting complete destruction of the one-party system. The Chinese market economy, because it is not democratically oriented, will require reorganization, which will lead to political instability. The situation may be complicated by the lack of a federal system and the pressure of unresolved national problems, resulting from the government's rejection a long time ago of the democratic right of nations for self-determination.

The Chinese opposition within the country and overseas considers the events in the former Soviet Union not as 'peaceful evolution' (*heping yanbian*), but as the rejection of a 'socialist heritage' discredited by history. It is seeking ways to democratize China by peaceful means, avoiding bloodshed and social disasters.

At the same time I believe that the concept of 'perfecting socialism' still prevails in the consciousness of the people at the mass level. This concept is used to explain the periodic failures in the task of realizing 'scientific socialism', and it is often suggested that there should be a return to the basics, a 'left' revision, to remedy these failures. This kind of Marxist fundamentalism is especially prevalent among the Party and among humanitarian intelligentsia who have already adopted the mood of opposition. It is only through distancing themselves from this concept, however, that it will be possible to prepare the ground for the removal of one-party 'socialist' dictates such as the New Economic Programme (which is doomed to failure, anyway), Khrushchev-type reforms of the kind which spread throughout Eastern Europe, and 'self-governing socialism' as in the former Yugoslavia.

I believe that the fate of the totalitarian model for the development of society in China will, in the end, be determined by the process of the degeneration and final extinction of China's current economic reforms. It is in precisely such a social context that I visualise the Chinese human rights movement, in close co-operation with other opposition forces both within the country and abroad, being able to uproot totalitarian despotism from its national soil and thereby bring to an end the four decades of anti-human government which China has suffered.

NOTES ON CONTRIBUTORS

JAY BERNSTEIN is Professor of Philosophy at the University of Essex. He is the author of: *The Philosophy of the Novel: Lukacs, Marxism and the Dialectics of Form* and *The Fate of Art*, and is completing a book entitled *The Ethics of Nonidentity: Critical Theory From Habermas to Adorno.*

LIU BINYAN trained as a journalist in China. He was purged in the Anti-Rightist Campaign of 1957 and after his rehabilitation in 1979 became an investigative reporter on *Renmin Ribao* [People's Daily]. He was purged again in 1987. He now lives in the United States.

LUCIE BOROTA is a lecturer in Chinese history at Charles University, Prague. Her research into Qing literati culture was carried out at the University of California at Berkeley.

HONG-MO CHAN is a theoretical physicist and a member of the *Alliance for a Better China*, based in Oxford.

TAMARA DRAGADZE is Research Fellow in the School of Slavonic and East European Studies, University of London.

YURI GARUSHYANTS is Senior Research Fellow of the China Modern History Research section, China Studies Department, Institute of Oriental Studies, Russian Academy of Social Sciences, Moscow. He has more than 200 publications on different issues of the modern history of China, and spent a year in the PRC after the events of June 4th 1989.

BONNIE S MCDOUGALL is Professor of Chinese at the University of Edinburgh, and the author of many books and articles on modern Chinese literature. Her recent translations include works by some of China's most notable figures from the 1980s: Bei Dao's poetry, Ah Cheng's fiction, and Chen Kaige's film *Yellow Earth.*

ANDREW J NATHAN is Professor of Political Science at Columbia University, New York, and author or co-author of *Chinese Democracy* (1985), *Human Rights in Contemporary China* (1986), and *China's Crisis* (1990).

MICHAEL SCHOENHALS is a researcher at Stockholm University, Sweden and the author of *Doing Things with Words in Chinese Politics: Five Studies* (University of California Institute of East Asian Studies, Berkeley, 1992).

JAMES D SEYMOUR is Senior Research Scholar at Columbia University's East Asian Institute in New York. He has published extensively on Chinese politics and human rights and is currently working on a book about Tibetan politics in recent years.

WANG HAO has been a member of the Executive Council (Paris) of the Federation for a Democratic China since 1990. He was awarded a L.L.B. in 1988 at Beijing University and gained his D.Phil at Oxford in 1992.

SUSAN WHITFIELD was chair of *June 4th China Support* from 1991–92. She is an historian of China and is conducting research at the School of Oriental and African Studies, University of London.

INDEX

ABC *see Alliance for a Better China*
Ai Qing 83, 85
Albania 11
Alliance for a Better China, The (ABC) 14, 50
American Revolution 27
Amnesty International 19, 50, 53, 54
Anquan Bu [State Security Bureau] 105
Anti-Rightist Movement (1957–8) 66, 83, 101, 108
Arendt, Hannah 24–26, 27
army *see* People's Liberation Army
arrests 11, 44, 106
    of workers 44
'At the side of the road' *see* 'Daopang'

'Banzhu ren' [The Class Teacher] 86–7, 88
Barthes, Roland 76
BBC 97
Bei Dao 81–2, 84, 86, 87–88
Beijing 13, 67, 79, 80, 81, 105
Beijing Opera 79
Beijing shudian 64
Beijing University 87
Bentham, Jeremy 20
Berlin 101
Bianjibu de Gushi [Stories from the Editorial Board] 72
Bierman, Wolf 84
Birch, Cyril 73, 86
'Black Li and White Li' *see* 'Hei-bai Li'
blacklisting, of writers 82–83 *see also* censorship
blasphemy 63
Bo Yang 77
bourgeois humanism 39
brainwashing 85
Brecht, Bertolt 74
Britain 38, 74, 76, 78
Bulgaria 11
Burke, Edmund 20

CAD *see* Chinese Alliance for Democracy
Calfa, Marian 92
Canada 40, 41
Cankao xiaoxi [Reference News] 97
Cankao ziliao [Reference Materials] 97
capitalism 10, 42–3, 49, 52, 61, 65–6, 71, 72, 75, 94, 95
Catholic Church 104
CBOs *see* Community Based Organizations

INDEX

JUNE 4TH CHINA SUPPORT is a group of individuals closely associated with China through work, study, trade and friendship. It was established after the events of June 4th, 1989 with the following aims • To provide humanitarian aid to those who have suffered injury, bereavement, loss of employment or personal hardship as a result of the June events • To provide counselling and financial assistance to those who may need to prolong their stay in Britain • To gather information on events leading up to and following June 4th 1989 in order to promote a well-documented and balanced view of the events and their significance • To secure the release of and prevent the execution of those arrested solely for their peaceful participation in the democracy movement • To keep the government and the people of Britain informed of the significance of these events for the future of Hong Kong and China. JUNE 4TH CHINA SUPPORT sponsors and patrons include David Blunkett MP, Lord Briggs, John Gittings, Jonathan Mirsky, Joseph Needham, Colin Thubron and Frances Wood. JUNE 4TH CHINA SUPPORT welcomes new members willing to assist in promoting its aims, and has a continuing requirement for financial support. If you wish to help in any way please contact:

JUNE 4TH CHINA SUPPORT, PO Box 190, London WC1X 9RL.